Bomber Command
Airfields of
Lincolnshire

Bomber Command Airfields of Lincolnshire

Peter Jacobs

Pen & Sword
AVIATION

First published in Great Britain in 2016 by
Pen & Sword Aviation
An imprint of Pen & Sword Books Ltd
47 Church Street
Barnsley
South Yorkshire
S70 2AS

Copyright © Peter Jacobs 2016

ISBN 978 1 78346 334 3

A CIP catalogue record for this book is
available from the British Library

Typeset in 10pt Palatino by Mac Style, Driffield, East Yorkshire
Printed and bound in the UK by CPI Group (UK) Ltd,
Croydon, CRO 4YY

Pen & Sword Books Ltd incorporates the Imprints of Pen &
Sword Aviation, Pen & Sword Maritime, Pen & Sword Military,
Wharncliffe Local History, Pen & Sword Select, Pen & Sword
Military Classics, Leo Cooper, Remember When, Seaforth
Publishing and Frontline Publishing

For a complete list of Pen & Sword titles please contact
PEN & SWORD BOOKS LIMITED
47 Church Street, Barnsley, South Yorkshire, S70 2AS, England
E-mail: enquiries@pen-and-sword.co.uk
Website: www.pen-and-sword.co.uk

Contents

Acknowledgements

This is the fourth book I have written on airfields during the Second World War as part of the *Aviation Heritage Trail* series, but the first to include the airfields of Bomber Command and the first involving the county of Lincolnshire. However, it is not the first time I have written about Bomber Command. Indeed, the very first article I wrote was about Bomber Command and so I must first take this opportunity to thank four people who helped get me started in this fascinating world of writing.

For many years, Peter Brown ran the Gossiper column in the *Lincolnshire Echo*. His column featured short accounts, usually of bygone days, written by the paper's readers for others to enjoy. I remember writing to Peter in 1990 after reading about Bomber Command's disastrous raid against Nuremberg on the night of 30/31 March 1944 and having been shocked by the appalling losses suffered that night (ninety-five bombers failed to return). My brief article was merely to raise awareness of the raid and was timed to be printed (assuming it would be printed) to coincide with its anniversary. Having sent in my article, I bought the paper on the night in eager anticipation at seeing my first piece of work in print; but it had not made the column. However, my disappointment did not last long and just days later I received a phone call from the *Echo* saying that my article had been received with interest and had given the paper an idea. I was asked to meet with the Editor, Cliff Smith, and the outcome from that meeting was me being asked to write a supplement for the *Lincolnshire Echo* as a tribute to Bomber Command and to mark the fiftieth anniversary of victory in the Battle of Britain. As I had no experience of writing, an RAF colleague of mine, Ken Delve, already an established military author, agreed to help and working closely with one of the *Echo*'s sub-editors, Peter Reynolds, *Wings of Glory* was produced. It was the first of many supplements that Peter and I went on to produce throughout the 1990s, including *Bomber County* (1996), a tribute to Bomber Command in Lincolnshire, while Ken and I went on to write *The Six-Year Offensive*, a book about Bomber Command during the Second World War (1992). And so that was how it all began. Since then I have gone on to write a number of books, including my first solo *The Lancaster Story* (1996), but I have never forgotten how it all started, and so I am glad to be able to thank Cliff Smith, Peter Brown, Peter Reynolds and Ken Delve for helping me through those early days.

There are a number of reasons why this latest book is special to me. Firstly, the majority of my RAF career was spent in Lincolnshire and so the county has now been my home for more than thirty years. Secondly, I have been fortunate to meet many Bomber Command veterans over the years, many of whom have shared with me their memories of wartime days. Furthermore, my home is built on the former wartime bomber airfield of RAF Skellingthorpe and so I became interested in its history and, particularly, those who flew from there during the Second World War. This led me to the 50 & 61 Squadrons Association and in 1991, I produced the Roll of Honour for the two squadrons, a book containing the 1,976 names of those who lost their lives during the Second World War. Then, as I found out more, it led to me writing *Bomb Aimer Over Berlin*, a book about the wartime experiences of Les Bartlett (2007), and from this publication came the invitation from Marshal of the Royal Air Force Sir Michael Beetham GCB CBE DFC AFC (Les's former wartime pilot), to write his biography *Stay The Distance* (2011).

From these brief explanations it can hopefully be seen that my interest in Bomber Command, its people and its airfields stretches back more than twenty-five years and so this latest publication is a natural progression from the stories I have been privileged to have already told. As a final comment on the 50 & 61 Squadrons Association, I have been its Chairman for the past twelve years. It only goes to show where an interest can lead!

As always, I have been helped by so many people during the course of my travels around the twenty-nine sites covered in this book. Those who require a special mention are: Group

Captain Jez Attridge (Station Commander) and the staff at the Battle of Britain Memorial Flight (RAF Coningsby); Andrew Stones (head teacher of the William Farr School), Brian Riley (Curator Heritage Centre) and Mrs Pat May (PA to head teacher) – all reference RAF Dunholme Lodge; the Panton family and volunteers at the Lincolnshire Aviation Heritage Centre (East Kirkby); staff at the Anglian Water Authority (Elsham Wolds); Colin Mitchell-Smith (Faldingworth Memorial Group); Jeremy Hayward (Fulbeck); the Church Warden at St Mary and St Peter in Ludford (Ludford Magna); the volunteers at the RAF Metheringham Airfield Visitor Centre; Wing Commander Mike Harrop (Station Commander) and the volunteers at the RAF Scampton Heritage Centre; Adrian Jones (Head Teacher of the Leslie Manser School – ref RAF Skellingthorpe); Group Captain Rich Barrow (Station Commander) and Wing Commander Colin Owen (RAF Waddington); and Anne Law (Curator RAF Wickenby Memorial Collection). But these are just the tip of an iceberg of people who help keep the stories of these once active bomber airfields alive, and so a big thank you to all those volunteers in communities and associations across the county who, for the past seventy years, have collectively preserved the history of the bomber airfields of Lincolnshire.

I must also thank Seb Cox and his staff at the Air Historical Branch (RAF) at RAF Northolt for their help over so many years. Where dates vary slightly between sources, particularly when it comes to the movement of squadrons between bases, I have used the dates in James J Halley's excellent book *Squadrons of the Royal Air Force and Commonwealth 1918–1988* – it is by far the best and most consistent record under one cover that I have found.

It only leaves me to say thank you to all those who served with Bomber Command during the Second World War. Without their remarkable contribution there would be no stories to be told. I must also thank the management and staff at Pen and Sword, and in particular Laura Hirst for all her effort behind the scenes to turn my work into the publication you see today.

Introduction

Across the county of Lincolnshire, there are some seventy sites of former airfields, which, at one time or another, have been part of the Royal Air Force's history. The vast majority, of course, no longer remain and today there are just a handful or so still in use by the RAF, but many others live on in a variety of ways.

Twenty-nine of these former airfields had a role to play with Bomber Command during the Second World War, and so it is easy to understand why Lincolnshire has since become known as Bomber County. The historic pattern of many of these airfields is much the same. Some came into existence during the First World War when there was a need for landing grounds as the number of aircraft serving with what was then the Royal Flying Corps increased. The flat terrain and vast open fields, with very few obstacles, as well as the soil, made Lincolnshire an ideal location for the development of these sites. This was particularly so in the central and southern parts of the county where there was less dense woodland, making the construction of airfields that much easier, and fewer industrial sites with resulting haze. The flat terrain also meant that ground communications between the many airfields popping up across the county was good. Furthermore, in the very early days, the Lincoln ridge meant that aircraft taking off into the prevailing westerly wind could quickly gain altitude, and one good example of a famous airfield to have been developed along the ridge during this period is Brattleby, later to become better known as RAF Scampton.

The old sites were somewhat primitive by later standards, and generally consisted of prepared strips of grass with tents for accommodation. In those days there were very few properly constructed buildings and when the First World War came to an

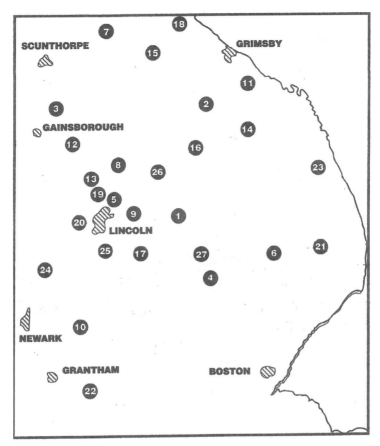

Lincolnshire's airfields of Bomber Command. Key: 1 – Bardney; 2 – Binbrook; 3 – Blyton; 4 – Coningsby; 5 – Dunholme Lodge; 6 – East Kirkby; 7 – Elsham Wolds; 8 – Faldingworth; 9 – Fiskerton; 10 – Fulbeck; 11 – Grimsby (Waltham); 12 – Hemswell; 13 – Ingham; 14 – Kelstern; 15 – Kirmington; 16 – Ludford Magna; 17 – Metheringham; 18 – North Killingholme; 19 – Scampton; 20 – Skellingthorpe; 21 – Spilsby; 22 – Spitalgate (Grantham); 23 – Strubby; 24 – Swinderby; 25 – Waddington; 26 – Wickenby; 27 – Woodhall Spa. Also included in this book for completeness are two training airfields at Sandtoft (to the south-west of Scunthorpe) and Sturgate (to the south-east of Gainsborough).

end, so too ended the brief lives of many of these early airfields with the land reverting to its pre-war use for agriculture.

While the origins of some airfields stem back to the First World War, most came along later following the birth, and then expansion, of RAF Bomber Command. Formed in 1936, one of the command's immediate problems was its lack of suitable airfields, especially in the north and east of England. With the possibility of war with Nazi Germany looming, Lincolnshire was considered ideal for the development of bomber airfields, not only because of all those reasons already mentioned but also because the county's position meant that the shortest route to and from most targets in Germany was by flying straight across the North Sea.

A programme to provide more airfields began but the requirement of the bombers at that time had changed little over the years; a suitable amount of grass plus space to erect a few hangars and buildings was all that was needed. Survey teams toured the country selecting sites and the purchase of land, or its lease, began.

Lincolnshire's former airfields were brought to life once more and more new sites were identified for use but, in many cases, work was slow in starting and by the time the contractors moved in the requirement was already changing. New bombers, such as the Vickers Wellington, introduced just before the Second World War, were heavier than their predecessors and so needed greater distance and a firmer surface from which to operate. Even by the time Britain went to war in September 1939, those bomber airfields that were ready to commence operations were still grass and although these would be suitable for the light bombers during the early days of hostilities, they would not be suitable for prolonged operations.

When the new and heavier four-engine aircraft, such as the Lancaster, arrived on the scene, the grass strips that were once suitable for bombers to operate, suddenly deteriorated and could not be used in bad weather. What was needed were airfields that could cope with the heavier bombers and runways that could sustain operations all-year round.

This change in requirement led to hardened runways and aircraft standings, all linked by a perimeter track, with new hangars and other buildings at the site. The standard pattern

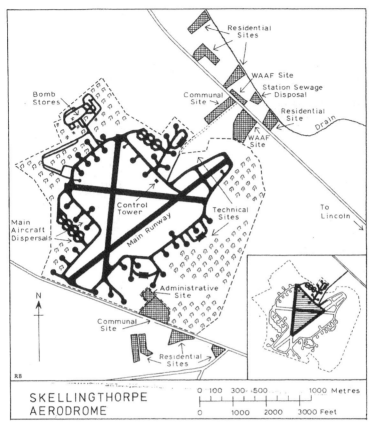

The introduction of heavier aircraft led to a change in requirement at Bomber Command's airfields with the construction of hardened runways and aircraft standings, all linked by a perimeter track, with new hangars and other buildings built on a number of sites. The standard pattern for a Class A airfield was three hardened runways – one main plus two secondary – constructed in an A-type, or triangular, pattern. The airfield layout shown here is that of RAF Skellingthorpe, near Lincoln, in 1944. (Author's collection)

for a Class A airfield of Bomber Command was three concrete/ tarmac runways – one main runway of around 2,000 yards in length plus two secondary runways, each around 1,400 yards – constructed in an A-type, or triangular, pattern. Also built on the airfields were hangars, of which there were many different types of structure (such as Type A, Type B, Type C, Bellman and

T2), depending on the site and materials available at the time, and varying domestic facilities ranging from Nissen huts to brick-constructed buildings.

Equipment at each airfield also varied but it was not until the later years of the war that landing aids appeared, such as FIDO (standing for 'Fog Investigation and Dispersal Operation', but sometimes referred to as 'Fog Intense Dispersal Operation' or 'Fog, Intense Dispersal Of'). With there often being a problem with fog or mist at airfields in Lincolnshire, FIDO was an ingenious method of dealing with poor visibility in the immediate vicinity of the runway. The system was based around a network of pipes filled with fuel and laid along the edges of the runway. In the case of poor visibility, the fuel was ignited and the effect was to lift the fog up to 300 feet, high enough to enable aircraft to land.

Depending mostly on their location, Lincolnshire's bomber airfields were allocated to either 1 Group or 5 Group of Bomber Command. Those airfields in the north of the county became part of 1 Group while those in the central and southern part of the county were allocated to 5 Group, although control of some of these airfields did change throughout the war. There were also changes to Bomber Command's organization as the war progressed and an administrative change within the command saw the introduction of a base system where airfields and their satellites (airfields used to support the main airfield's operations) were given a base number; an example being 14 Base, with Ludford Magna as the base headquarters and Wickenby and Faldingworth as its two satellites.

At the end of the Second World War many airfields reverted to their pre-war use, usually agricultural, although some have since been developed for housing or industry, while a handful were retained for military, commercial or private flying. Of those airfields that did survive the post-war cull to remain in use by the RAF, the wartime layout survived until well into the 1950s when the introduction of heavy jet bombers, such as the Vulcan, meant changes to the runway layout, taxiways and hard standings to take the extra weight and longer take-off runs of the new generation of aircraft.

Three of Lincolnshire's wartime bomber airfields – Coningsby, Scampton and Waddington – are still in use by the RAF today, while Kirmington is now Humberside Airport. But although others have long gone, there are often reminders still to be found. At East Kirkby, Hemswell, Metheringham and Wickenby, for example, much can still be seen today.

For each airfield I have identified the site and given details of how to find it, and briefly described its history in addition to explaining what happened there during the Second World War. I have also included brief details of anything of interest that remains at the site today and a summary of the operational squadrons that served at the airfield during the Second World War. Although three of the airfields – Sandtoft, Spitalgate and Sturgate – were never home to operational squadrons during the Second World War, they were used by aircraft of Bomber Command at some time or another during the war and so are included for completion.

But to set everything into context, I have firstly summarized Bomber Command during the Second World War. This will hopefully provide a useful background and set the scene for the rest of the book. As far as the airfields are concerned, I have divided the book into two, with all airfields shown as either part of 1 Group or 5 Group Bomber Command. There are occasions when the airfield transferred between the command's groups but to avoid duplication, the airfield is included under the group where it spent most of its time during the war. Within each part the airfields are presented in alphabetical order rather than to try and present them in any other way. Furthermore, because so many of Bomber Command's squadrons were involved in the same operations – such was the nature of the bombing campaigns – I have avoided repetition by choosing to tell certain stories through one airfield rather than cover the story of the same raid at every airfield involved. Only the limited space prevents me from writing more.

Whatever your interest, be it local or otherwise, there is a real mix of discoveries to be found. There can still be so much to see when driving around Lincolnshire, where the famous names of these once active bomber airfields remain. Enjoy the book!

Peter Jacobs

Bomber Command in the Second World War

The Second World War lasted almost six years and cost millions of lives. Yet only one force on the Allied side was continuously involved in active operations against Hitler's Nazi war machine – RAF Bomber Command.

When Bomber Command formed in July 1936, under its first Air Officer Commanding-in-Chief, Air Chief Marshal Sir John Steel, the Royal Air Force was going through a period of change. Its ageing biplanes were being replaced by faster and more modern aircraft and a series of pre-war RAF Expansion Schemes included the proposal for ninety squadrons with a total strength of 1,659 aircraft, although the expansion was not expected to be complete until 1943. There was also a gradual acceptance amongst the Air Staff towards the concept of fewer but more capable bombers, which would become central to Bomber Command planning. In simple terms, a squadron of fewer but heavier bombers could deliver a greater tonnage of bombs on target than a squadron consisting of a greater number of light bombers.

Germany's invasion of Poland on 1 September 1939 brought the RAF to increased readiness and then, on 3 September, with Britain's declaration of war with Germany, its bombers were fully armed and placed on immediate standby, ready to commence Bomber Command's first operations of the war; albeit the searches for German shipping over the North Sea that followed proved, in the main, fruitless.

Bomber Command had entered the Second World War with fifty-five squadrons spread across five operational groups: 1 Group (headquartered at Benson but later to be at Bawtry)

Hampdens pictured over Lincoln Cathedral during the early days of the war. (Author's collection via the Lincolnshire Echo)

equipped with Fairey Battles; 2 Group (Wyton) with Bristol Blenheims; 3 Group (Mildenhall) was equipped with Vickers Wellingtons; 4 Group (Linton-on-Ouse) operated Armstrong Whitworth Whitleys; and 5 Group, equipped with Handley Page Hampdens, was based mostly at airfields in Lincolnshire with its headquarters at St Vincent's Hall in Grantham, although this would later be moved to Morton Hall near Swinderby.

With 1 Group's Battle squadrons sent to France as part of the Advanced Air Striking Force, which would lead to the temporary disbandment of the group until the campaign was over, it was left to the Wellingtons, Whitleys and Hampdens to bear the brunt of Bomber Command's early campaign. But, with the exception of the Wellington, these aircraft were soon to be found lacking in a modern air war. In simple and practical terms, Bomber Command was not equipped for the role it was assigned; it was not large enough to operate as a strategic independent bombing force, its technological capability was lacking and bombing methods still lacked accuracy. Furthermore, the political constraints placed on the bomber crews during the early months of the war prevented attacks against any German targets except for its naval fleet.

It took the loss of twelve Wellingtons over Wilhelmshaven on 18 December 1939 (half the force dispatched) for the strategists to realize that the bombers could not survive in daylight. The intervention of German fighters off the German coast had resulted in disaster and these losses came just four days after an earlier attempt to attack enemy shipping when five of twelve Wellingtons were lost to enemy flak and fighters. But switching to operating at night would not be easy. The aircraft were not equipped to navigate in the dark and their crews were not trained to operate at night.

For the next three months there was no great change in bombing strategy. Then, following a German raid against the Royal Navy at Scapa Flow in March 1940, where bombs had been dropped on land, killing one civilian and wounding several more, Bomber Command was ordered to carry out a reprisal raid on a German seaplane base on the southernmost tip of the island of Sylt in northern Germany. The raid that followed, involving thirty Whitleys and twenty Hampdens, was Bomber Command's first real bombing raid of the war but despite the crews claiming success, post-raid reconnaissance revealed no damage and provided further evidence of the difficulty of operating at night.

Germany's invasion of France and the Low Countries during May 1940 brought a change in bombing strategy and now permitted the bombing of targets east of the Rhine, particularly the industrial heartland of Germany, the Ruhr. Then, when

France fell, and with Britain facing the increasing threat of Nazi invasion during the summer of 1940, Bomber Command's target list was revised to include enemy ports and shipping, including the mass of invasion barges that were appearing in large numbers across the Channel. And when German bombs fell on London during the night of 24/25 August, the British Prime Minister, Winston Churchill, ordered Bomber Command to carry out an immediate retaliatory raid on Berlin.

The following night a force of more than fifty Wellingtons and Hampdens took part in the raid. Thick cloud over the German capital made identification of targets all but impossible but bombs were dropped. Although the results from this first bombing raid against the Nazi capital were poor, the raid had made an important point; not only to Hitler but also to the people of Germany. By the end of the month Berlin had been attacked twice more.

While Bomber Command's raids were increasing in size, there was still no appetite to concentrate its effort against a single target on any one night. But that changed on the night of 23/24 September 1940 when Bomber Command sent a main force of 129 aircraft – a mix of Hampdens, Wellingtons and Whitleys – to Berlin with some success. However, despite great effort from those within Bomber Command, the first year of war had achieved little in the way of bombing success. There had, of course, been a huge psychological impact on both sides of the Channel and, at the very least, Bomber Command had shown that Britain was far from defeated and was capable of hitting back.

Britain's economic warfare experts had already concluded that oil was key to the German war machine and so the offensive against oil synthetic plants and other related targets was increased. In early February 1941 the first of the RAF's new and heavier bombers, the Short Stirling, entered service and by the end of the month, the second, the Avro Manchester, had also made its operational debut. Then, the following month, the third, the Handley Page Halifax, took part in its first operations.

Things were looking up but Bomber Command was suddenly diverted away from its main effort to support the Battle of the Atlantic, a campaign that would last for four months before the main offensive against targets in Germany resumed during the summer of 1941. But there were still problems as far as bombing accuracy was concerned. Even after nearly two years of war, only one bomb in ten was estimated to have fallen within five miles (eight kilometres) of its intended target. However, it would be some time before navigation and bombing techniques were improved and so, for now, the priority was to destroy German industry and dislocate its transportation system, as well as breaking the morale of the civil population as a whole and, in particular, the industrial workers.

As 1941 drew to a close, Bomber Command spread its effort throughout the Ruhr and to a number of German cities and towns. It remained the only offensive weapon the British had and, fortunately, Churchill, in the absence of an alternative, supported its expansion. However, Bomber Command could still only muster fifty-six squadrons, of which only one-quarter consisted of the newer and heavier bombers. The RAF still lacked enough bombers and the capability to win a decisive strategic bombing campaign.

For Bomber Command, 1942 would prove to be a crucial year and marked a turning point in its fortunes. In February, and after frequent changes of commander, Bomber Command appointed as its head the man who was to inspire and lead it for the rest of the war – Air Marshal Arthur Harris. His appointment came at a time when the command's morale was probably at its lowest ebb and coincided with a scathing report about its inability to achieve the tasks it had been set.

Expansion was to be one of Harris's priorities. He had a total of just over 500 aircraft, of which the vast majority were operating at night. These were the Wellingtons, Hampdens, Whitleys, Stirlings, Halifaxes and Manchesters. He also had a number of Blenheims and Bostons used only by day, although these made up just 7 per cent of his total force. Harris immediately set about the shortage of suitable aircraft and to improve the efficiency of navigation aids and bombing techniques. He knew that expansion would rely on having enough crews ready to take part in operations, which meant an increase in the training establishments with each group responsible for the training of its own bomber crews. This would see the creation of a number of heavy conversion units (HCUs) to bridge the gap between the

In February 1942, Bomber Command appointed Air Marshal Arthur Harris as its head. His appointment had come at a time when morale was probably at its lowest ebb, but Harris would inspire and lead Bomber Command for the rest of the war. (AHB)

twin-engine Wellington used in training and the heavier four-engine bombers now entering operational service.

Within two weeks of Harris's arrival the four-engine Avro Lancaster made its operational debut. It was the last of the four-engine heavies to arrive in service but it would go on to become the best and by far the most capable of them all. But with Bomber Command's expansion there were not enough pilots to sustain two pilots within a bomber crew and so a new crew position was introduced to the heavy bombers to relieve the pilot of the many tasks he had. This was the flight engineer and many of the early volunteers came from ground personnel across the squadrons, bringing the Lancaster crew, for example, to seven: pilot; navigator; flight engineer; bomb aimer; and a wireless operator/air gunner in addition to the two air gunners in the mid-upper and rear turrets. Volunteers came from all across the Commonwealth with an operational tour generally considered to be thirty operational sorties.

1942 would prove to be a crucial year for Bomber Command and marked a turning point in its fortunes. The Avro Lancaster was the last of the four-engine heavies to arrive in service but it would go on to become the best and by far the most capable of them all. (AHB)

The introduction of the Lancaster allowed Harris to explore its true capability and to show the Nazi leadership that Bomber Command could hit any target at any time. This capability was first demonstrated in April 1942 when two of Lincolnshire's squadrons carried out a daring low level daylight raid against a factory at Augsburg. Although it proved costly, as so many of these specialist raids sadly did, Bomber Command had made a significant statement in the air war over Germany.

Harris was also keen to show doubters within the other services, as well as his own, that a bombing campaign, if conducted properly, would help bring an end to hostilities. He soon had enough assets to mount by far the biggest raid of the war and this took place against Germany's third largest city of Cologne at the end of May 1942. It was Harris's 'Thousand-Bomber' plan, something he had long wanted to carry out, and using all available resources, including aircraft and instructors from the command's many training units, 1,047 bombers were made available for the raid.

For the record, this first Thousand-Bomber raid was considered a success, although a follow-up mass effort two nights later, this time against Essen, was not. Harris knew that he could not hold on to such large numbers of aircraft for long and with the moon period over the aircraft and crews returned to normal operations and training duties. But there was still time for a third all-out effort towards the end of June when more than a thousand bombers, including aircraft from Coastal Command and a handful from Army Co-Operation Command, attacked Bremen. It was the RAF's largest raid of the war. Bomber Command had never before dispatched such a large and mixed force, nor would it ever do so again.

The three Thousand-Bomber raids show just how far Bomber Command had come in just a few months. The next thing was to improve navigation and bombing techniques, and this led to the formation of the Path Finder Force (PFF) in August 1942 under the command of Group Captain (later Air Vice-Marshal) Donald Bennett. But the idea had divided opinions within Bomber Command. While it was difficult to argue against having a trained force to find and mark targets, there was opposition to having what would be perceived to be an elite force within the command. Besides, the group commanders were reluctant to give up their best crews. In the end, the initial composition of the PFF brought together squadrons from each of the bomber groups.

The PFF was soon to become part of 8 Group and proved its worth, albeit at a heavy cost to its crews, and its introduction coincided with the first American heavy bomber operations over Europe. Bomber Command now had a daylight partner in a combined strategic bombing offensive against Nazi Germany.

While the past year had been one of critical expansion, 1943 was to be a crucial year for Bomber Command as it was to be the first year that it could deliver the long-promised destructive power and with previously unheard of accuracy. The technical war had been developing at pace but two early systems to be introduced, called Gee (an electronic aid to assist navigation and to permit blind-bombing) and Oboe (probably the most accurate navigation aid to be introduced during the war), relied on ground stations and could be jammed. What was needed was an airborne system, independent of ground stations, and this had led to the development of an airborne radar system called H2S. Being an airborne system, H2S had no limitation of range and, it was thought, would not be jammed. Although that would ultimately prove not to be the case, it was a major step forward and although it was not without its problems, H2S had many advantages over the ground-based systems.

With such improvements in technology and the introduction of the Pathfinders, overall bombing accuracy improved and far better results were achieved during the first quarter of 1943. It was estimated that the combination of Oboe and H2S had increased bombing accuracy three-fold at least. But as the RAF's technology and night tactics continued to evolve, so did the Luftwaffe's and German night fighter crews were also achieving much success. The introduction of the *Lichtenstein* radar, with its complex *Matratze* (mattress) of antennas, and the development of *Schräge Musik* (taken from the German colloquialism for 'Jazz Music'), a system using twin upward-firing cannons, had introduced a new fear to the crews of Bomber Command. The night fighter no longer had to approach the bomber from the stern but could now slowly approach from beneath until in a position to open fire. The combination of *Lichtenstein* and *Schräge Musik* had turned the German night fighter into an extremely effective weapon and Bomber Command losses continued to mount. The night war had become a hard and, at times, horrific campaign for both sides.

No summary of Bomber Command during the Second World War would be complete without mentioning the daring low-level night attack against the Ruhr Dams by 617 Squadron, better known since as the 'Dambusters', in May 1943. The legendary raid was carried out from the Lincolnshire airfield of Scampton and resulted in its leader, Wing Commander Guy Gibson, and the designer of the 'bouncing bomb', Barnes Wallis, becoming household names overnight. The bouncing bomb was an ingenious design and the breaching of two dams an outstanding feat of flying and courage. But success had come at a cost with the loss of fifty-three lives.

The Battle of the Ruhr was followed by the Battle of Hamburg, a short campaign lasting less than two weeks in the summer of 1943. But the Battle of Berlin that followed, which began in earnest in November and lasted until the end of March 1944,

By the end of 1943, small
bombs such as the 500 lb
and 1000 lb general purpose
bombs, although still very
much in use, had been
surpassed in design and
capability by bombs such as
the 2,000 lb armour-piercing
bomb, used against ships
and dockyards, and the
4,000 lb high-capacity bomb,
known as the 'Cookie'. The
Lancaster proved an ideal
aircraft for carrying mixed
bomb loads depending on the
task. (AHB)

during which there were no fewer than sixteen major raids
against the Nazi capital, proved to be the toughest and costliest
campaign of all. Over 9,000 sorties were flown against Berlin
with the loss of more than 500 aircraft. And if that was not bad
enough, Bomber Command suffered its heaviest losses in one
night during a raid against Nuremberg on the last night of
March 1944; ninety-five bombers were lost from the attacking
force of nearly 800 aircraft. It marked a period of success for
the Luftwaffe's night fighters and Harris's belief that Germany
could be defeated by sustained bombing alone had not proved
to be the case.

Still licking its wounds following the hard winter of 1943/44,
Bomber Command turned its attention to supporting the build-
up towards the Allied landings in Europe, which took place on
6 June 1944, D-Day, and as the Allies pushed further towards

Germany, Bomber Command's losses began to fall; aided by the fact that Allied fighters were starting to rule the sky over Europe as Germany's once invincible war machine became stretched across several fronts.

Bomber Command's tactics had continued to evolve. A Master Bomber was there to direct bombing operations over the target and bombing techniques had improved, not only because of technology but also because bombs had got bigger and more capable. Small bombs such as the 500 lb and 1,000 lb general purpose bombs, although still very much in use, had been surpassed in capability by bombs such as the 2,000 lb armour-piercing bomb, used against ships and dockyards, and the 4,000 lb high-capacity bomb, known as the 'Cookie'. This latter bomb was designed with a cylindrical, mild steel casing, filled with high explosive, and either a conical- or dome-shaped nose fitted with either an impact or delayed fuse, and filled with Amatol, Minol or Tritonal, for use against tactical targets such as large industrial sites. Next up was the 8,000 lb high-capacity bomb, best described as two Cookies' worth, with either an impact or

Operations required the efforts of countless men and women from the many trades of the RAF's ground personnel. Shown here is a refuelling bowser and ground crew of 12 Squadron at Wickenby during 1944. (RAF Wickenby Memorial Collection via Anne Law)

barometric fuse and used for the demolition of targets such as large and heavily industrialized areas. Then came the 12,000 lb high capacity bomb and the 12,000 lb 'Tallboy'. The HC variant was similar in principle to the 4,000 lb and 8,000 lb bombs but the Tallboy was a quite different bomb altogether. Designed by Barnes Wallis, it was an earthquake bomb and was introduced during 1944 to bring down strategically important targets, such as viaducts, and to penetrate particularly hardened or underground targets, such as U-boat pens, railway tunnels and V-weapon sites that were rapidly appearing in the Pas de Calais and causing terror in southern England. Because of its size, fins had to be fitted to the Tallboy to stabilize the bomb and the Lancaster had to be modified to carry it. But even this monstrous design would be surpassed by the 22,000 lb Grand Slam, another earthquake bomb similar in design and appearance to the Tallboy but containing 11,000 lb of Torpex D and used against exceptionally strong targets. To carry this huge weapon required a specially modified Lancaster and the first Grand Slam was dropped just weeks before the end of the war. Bombing had come a long way and the Lancaster had given Bomber Command, and the Allies, a true strategic bombing capability.

There is probably no one individual who sums up the courage of those who served with Bomber Command during the Second World War more than Wing Commander Guy Gibson VC DSO* DFC*. At the age of just twenty-four, Gibson led the daring raid on the Ruhr Dams in May 1943 but was sadly killed in September 1944, while on a ground tour, after volunteering for one more operation as Master Bomber against Rheydt and Mönchengladbach. (AHB)

The last major raid of the war took place on 25 April 1945 when a force of Lancasters and Mosquitos attacked Hitler's Berghof (the Eagle's Nest) and SS barracks at Berchtesgaden in the Bavarian Alps. Then, as the war in Europe drew to a close, Bomber Command carried out Operation *Manna*, the dropping of food supplies to the civilian population of Holland. More than 3,000 sorties were flown in the last days of April and early May 1945, during which aircraft dropped some 7,000 tons of food. Then, with hostilities in Europe over, Bomber Command carried out Operation *Exodus*, the repatriation of Allied prisoners of war. Lancasters were adapted to carry up to twenty-five passengers and some 3,000 round-trips were flown throughout May, returning 74,000 prisoners of war. Finally, Bomber Command carried out Operation *Dodge* to bring home the British Eighth Army from Italy and the Central Mediterranean.

Throughout its six-year offensive during the Second World War, Bomber Command had flown more than 360,000 missions and had played a vital role in the Allied victory. But it had come at a huge cost. The Bomber Command Memorial in Green Park, London, pays tribute to the 55,573 who died while serving with the command. Nearly 10,000 more became prisoners of war and nearly as many again were either wounded in action or injured in flying accidents. It is no coincidence that of the thirty-two Victoria Crosses awarded to airman during the Second World War, nineteen were awarded to men of Bomber Command.

PART I

Airfields of 1 Group: North Lincolnshire

CHAPTER ONE

Binbrook

The name of Binbrook has written its own place in the history of Lincolnshire airfields. In post-war years it was one of the RAF's Cold War fighter airfields and home to supersonic Lightnings, but it was as a bomber airfield that Binbrook was built and first opened in 1940 as part of 1 Group Bomber Command.

Binbrook's location high up on the Lincolnshire Wolds had made it ideal for development as a bomber airfield. But when war broke out in September 1939, Binbrook was far from ready for operations, and it was a further nine months before the airfield was ready to receive its first aircraft.

At that stage the airfield was of basic design, with grass runways, but by July 1940 Binbrook was considered sufficiently ready to receive the Fairey Battle light bombers of 12 and 142 Squadrons that had returned from the RAF's Advanced Air Striking Force in France. The two squadrons had suffered losses in the short but costly campaign and were in need of a rest and to regroup before returning to operations.

Despite being at Binbrook for a so-called rest, a crew of 12 Squadron were to become 1 Group's first casualties of the war. On 1 August a Battle was returning from a sortie over the North Sea after looking for enemy shipping when it was accidentally shot down by RAF fighters off Mablethorpe. The crew – Flying Officer Brian Moss (pilot), 23-year-old Sergeant Brian Long (observer) and Sergeant Thomas Radley (wireless operator) – are all buried in Binbrook's (St Mary and St Gabriel) churchyard.

The threat of Nazi invasion meant that both Battle squadrons were needed in the south where the struggle for Britain's survival was raging, but both soon returned to Binbrook and in September began preparations to receive Wellington bombers.

Despite being sent to Binbrook for a so-called rest, a crew of 12 Squadron were to become 1 Group's first casualties of the war. On 1 August a Battle was returning from a sortie over the North Sea after looking for enemy shipping when it was accidentally shot down by RAF fighters off Mablethorpe. The crew – Flying Officer Brian Moss (pilot), 23-year-old Sergeant Brian Long (observer) and Sergeant Thomas Radley (wireless operator) – are buried in Binbrook's (St Mary and St Gabriel) churchyard. (Author)

With a crew of six (two pilots, an observer, two wireless operators/air gunners and a rear gunner), the Wellington Mk II would be at the forefront of Bomber Command's operations during the early years of the war. But the combination of operating a heavier aircraft from a grass airfield and poor weather during the winter of 1940/41 meant there were occasions when the squadrons were unable to fly. Any amount of rain soon saturated the grass runways, which was not helped by the fact that the airfield had been built in an area of dip on the higher slopes of the Wolds, and the airfield often turned to mud. There was also much snow and ice during the winter, making operating from the airfield all but impossible.

The Lincolnshire weather had done nothing to help the squadrons convert to their new type but following an extensive work-up, and a period of better weather, Wellington operations began in the spring of 1941. On the night of 9/10 April, seven of Binbrook's aircraft took part in a raid against Emden. The raid was one of a number of minor operations carried out that night to divert the enemy's defences from Bomber Command's main effort against Berlin. Four of the Wellingtons taking part were from 12 Squadron, including that flown by the squadron commander, 34-year-old Wing Commander Vyvian Blackden. Sadly, one failed to return; that of Blackden. It was a sad loss for the squadron and for Binbrook.

At that stage of the war there were only a dozen or so Wellingtons at the airfield. It was early days but there was little or no co-ordination between squadrons or other airfields. The Binbrook crews would be given their target and time for take-off, plus their bomb load, but, other than that were essentially left to plan their own raid.

The two squadrons worked hard to help carry the bombing offensive to Germany and gradually the number of Wellingtons available each night increased, and soon each squadron was able to send a dozen or so aircraft a night on ops.

During this period Binbrook was also home to the Lysanders of 1 Group's Target-Towing Flight. These had arrived the previous September but the flight was now re-named 1481 Target Towing & Gunnery Flight. During the following months the flight's establishment would be boosted by the addition of twin-engine

Wellingtons of 12 Squadron pictured at Binbrook one night in February 1942.
(RAF Wickenby Memorial Collection via Anne Law)

Whitleys, and then Wellingtons, and although these aircraft were used for training purposes, they would occasionally be used for operations when needed, such as during Bomber Command's three Thousand-Bomber raids. The Whitleys would eventually be phased out of service to be replaced by single-engine Miles Martinet towing tugs, which, in turn, were later replaced by Hawker Hurricanes and the flight absorbed into 1687 Flight headquartered at Ingham.

As the winter of 1941 drew closer it was important to ensure the onset of bad weather would not again halt operational flying from Binbrook. The airfield was now in desperate need of repair and improvement. In particular, it needed hardened runways and hard standings but it would be several months before it was the airfield's turn for modification and improvements. With the real possibility that it would not be possible to maintain nightly operations from the airfield throughout the coming winter, 142 Squadron moved to Grimsby in November 1941, leaving 12 Squadron to operate from Binbrook alone and to continue the nightly struggle for what would be nearly another year.

The squadron lost another commanding officer on the night of 26/27 March 1942 when the highly decorated Wing Commander Albert Golding, twice awarded the Distinguished Flying Cross (DFC), failed to return from a raid against the Krupp steel

Binbrook today. Much of the former airfield has survived, although most buildings are now derelict. (Author)

factories at Essen. His aircraft was one of ten Wellingtons lost from the raiding force of more than a hundred aircraft. Golding's aircraft was shot down over Holland; all six of the crew were killed.

At the end of May the squadron sent all available Wellingtons, twenty-eight aircraft in all, to Cologne on the first Thousand-Bomber raid. Then, on the night of 27/28 August, Binbrook suffered its heaviest losses of the war during a raid against Kassel. More than 300 bombers of all types were involved, including thirty-six Wellingtons from Binbrook. Bombing conditions were generally good with little cloud over the target area and the Pathfinders had marked the target well. Damage to Kassel was reported to be widespread but nine of Binbrook's Wellingtons failed to return.

Tragically, seventeen more aircraft were to be lost during the first three weeks of September, bringing the squadron's losses to nearly fifty during the past three months. 12 Squadron now moved out to Wickenby, a new airfield, and 1481 Flight moved to Blyton so that Binbrook could finally get the improvements the airfield so desperately required.

Flying stopped from Binbrook until May 1943 when the airfield was considered ready to receive the first of its four-engine Lancaster heavy bombers that were now serving with Bomber Command. This brought the Australians of 460 (RAAF) Squadron to Binbrook. The different uniforms and strange accents soon became the topic of conversation within the Lincolnshire Wolds but it was the start of a remarkable friendship between the Australians and the village of Binbrook that would last to this day.

Within days of moving in to Binbrook the Aussies were in action. There had been a nine-day break in major operations over Germany, during which 617 Squadron carried out the legendary Dams raid (see the account of the raid under Scampton), but, on the night of 23/24 May 1943, Bomber Command was back in full swing. More than 800 bombers were sent to Dortmund, including twenty-four Lancasters of 460 (RAAF) Squadron. The raid proved a success but two of 460's aircraft were amongst the thirty-eight bombers that failed to return.

Binbrook was now commanded by 28-year-old Group Captain Hughie Edwards. Born in Freemantle, Western

Australia, Edwards was already a highly decorated pilot. Flying the Blenheim, he had first been awarded the DFC before he was awarded the Victoria Cross for leading a daring low-level daylight raid against Bremen in July 1941. Then, after serving in Malta, he had flown the Mosquito and was awarded the Distinguished Service Order (DSO) for leading more daring raids. Although Edwards was now the station commander at Binbrook and primarily filling an administrative post, he would continue to fly on operations with 460 (RAAF) Squadron whenever he could.

As part of the re-organization of Bomber Command during 1943, Binbrook was designated the Headquarters of 12 Base, under the overall command of the legendary Air Commodore Arthur Wray (see Hemswell and Grimsby for more information about Wray), with his responsibilities including the administration and running of the nearby airfields at Kelstern and Grimsby. Wray was a regular visitor to both and it is hardly surprising that he tried to fly on operations whenever possible during his time at Binbrook. But as an air commodore his wish was met with fierce opposition from his superiors, although he did manage to convert to the Lancaster and he is known to have flown at least two operational sorties during this time.

The first of these extra ops was a raid to Hamburg on the night of 29/30 July 1943. Always keen to pass on his knowledge and experience to the younger crews under his command, Wray flew to Hamburg with a brand new crew. The crew had only completed their conversion training that morning and so had never been on operations or under fire before. At the age of forty-seven, Wray took the 'sprog' crew on their first op and brought them back safely. It was an example of Wray's quite remarkable leadership and personal determination to operate against the enemy, for which he was awarded the DSO. But the hugely inspirational Wray, seemingly loved by all of his crews, would have to wait until March 1944 for his next op, which he flew from Grimsby, after which it appears he was finally 'grounded' by his group commander. Placed on the Retired List after the war, Wray became an accomplished glider pilot. In 1972, after a long and exhausting cross-country flight of nearly 200 miles and lasting five hours, he touched down at Binbrook for the last time, earning him the international 'Gold C.' badge, a coveted distinction in the gliding world, at the age of seventy-five. The RAF station of Binbrook gave the legendary Air Commodore Arthur Wray DSO MC DFC* AFC a wonderful party to welcome the legendary airman home.

Simply by their presence, the likes of Arthur Wray and Hughie Edwards did so much to boost morale at Binbrook during a time when losses were high. Edwards would remain at Binbrook until the end of 1944 when he was posted to the Far East, and during his time as station commander it is believed that he flew on at least fifteen operations.

The winter of 1943/44 witnessed the Battle of Berlin, the hardest campaign of them all and a costly one for 460 (RAAF) Squadron. The squadron flew nearly 400 ops against the capital during the lengthy campaign at a cost of twenty-eight aircraft with the loss of more than 130 lives; the worst night being 2/3 December 1943 when five of the squadron's twenty-five aircraft were lost after incorrectly forecast winds and waiting night fighters caused havoc amongst the attacking force. Included in the many killed that night were two newspaper reporters that had been given special permission to fly with the squadron on the raid.

The hard campaign against Berlin was followed by the disastrous raid against Nuremberg at the end of March 1944. Amongst the ninety-five bombers lost that night were three from Binbrook and one of those killed was Pilot Officer Arthur Chadwick-Bates; it was to have been the last trip of his operational tour. He was the rear gunner to Squadron Leader Eric Utz, a holder of two DFCs who was also killed; it was Utz's forty-ninth op.

Binbrook became home to 1 Group's own specialist Pathfinder unit during the spring of 1944. Called the 1 Group Special Duties Flight under the command of Squadron Leader Bill Breakspear, the flight consisted of six Lancasters and was made up of some of the group's most experienced crews drawn from a number of 1 Group's airfields. The flight made its operational debut on the night of 30 April 1944 when it marked the target at Maintenon, the Luftwaffe's largest ammunition dump in northern France. The result was a successful raid by more than a hundred of the group's Lancasters, with the arms dump hit without causing damage to the surrounding area.

By this time Bomber Command was involved in softening up the enemy defences in northern France and cutting vital lines of communications. It was a crucial phase of preparing the ground for the forthcoming Allied landings of north-west Europe and these raids often proved costly. One of 460's worst nights was on 3/4 May 1944 when five of its seventeen Lancasters taking part in a raid against a German military camp near the French village of Mailly-le-Camp failed to return. It was also a costly raid for Bomber Command. Of nearly 350 Lancasters that took part, forty-two were lost (12 per cent of the attacking force).

Over the following weeks and months, 460 continued to support the Allied landings. As the Luftwaffe resistance weakened, mainly due to the Allies now being able to provide fighter escort for its bombers, many sorties were being flown during the day.

One of 460's Lancasters worthy of special mention during this period is W4783 'AR-G George', a Mk I built by Metropolitan-Vickers Limited in Manchester during 1942, which was retired from operations after its ninetieth op and later flown to Australia where it has since been on display at the museum at the Australian War Memorial in Canberra. The aircraft had flown its first operation in December 1942 and had survived intact until April 1944 but given the high losses being suffered by the Aussies at that time, the chances of 'G-George' completing a further ten ops to become a centurion were considered unlikely. Many Australians had safely returned from operations in this legendary aircraft, including Flight Sergeant James Saint-Smith, a young pilot from New South Wales. He flew 'G-George' on at least thirteen operations during his tour with 460 in 1943 and was awarded the Distinguished Flying Medal (DFM). He was later commissioned and awarded the DFC, but 26-year-old Saint-Smith was killed in June 1944 while flying a Mosquito of 627 Squadron from Woodhall Spa.

Binbrook remained home to the Australians for the rest of the war. During its two years at the airfield, 460 (RAAF) Squadron had flown more than 6,000 sorties and had dropped nearly 25,000 tons of bombs but, sadly, it had come at a cost of more than a thousand aircrew casualties; the highest of any Australian squadron during the war.

The memorial to 460 (RAAF) Squadron can be found when entering Binbrook village from the Market Rasen direction, opposite the sharp left turn (Orford Road) towards the former airfield. (Author)

In Binbrook's five years at war, more than 270 aircraft had failed to return from operations with the loss of around 1,200 lives. With hostilities over, 460 (RAAF) Squadron moved to East Kirkby where it disbanded soon after. However, the future of Binbrook was bright as it was one of the few bomber airfields in Lincolnshire to be retained by the post-war RAF. The Lancasters of 12 Squadron returned in September and by 1946 the number of squadrons at Binbrook had risen to four.

The Lancasters were gradually replaced by Avro Lincolns, which, in turn, were replaced by the new Canberra bomber as part of the RAF's conversion to the jet age. Four Canberra squadrons operated from the airfield in the 1950s, during which they took part in overseas operations such as Suez and Malaya, as well as several exercises and visits worldwide as the RAF began a new era of conducting long-range operations. But by the end of the decade all the squadrons had either disbanded or moved out in preparation for receiving the new Avro Vulcan as part of the RAF's build-up of the V-Force.

By the beginning of 1960, Binbrook had closed to flying and was put on care and maintenance before the airfield transferred to Fighter Command. Following an extension to the main runway and other developments, the airfield was used briefly by a number of different fighter types, including Javelins, Meteors and Canberras, before, in 1965, Binbrook welcomed the RAF's newest supersonic fighter, the Lightning.

Binbrook was home to the Lightning for more than twenty years, after which it closed to flying, but in 1990 the airfield was used for filming *Memphis Belle*, a fictionalization of a 1944 documentary film that provides an account of the final mission of the crew of a B-17 Flying Fortress, which in May 1943 became the first American Air Force heavy bomber to complete twenty-five missions over Europe and was then returned to the United States. The 1990 version is appropriately dedicated to all airmen, friend or foe, who fought in the skies above Europe during the Second World War.

Binbrook remains one of the most famous of Lincolnshire's airfields, having enjoyed a distinguished history as both a bomber and fighter base. The former airfield can be found about seven miles to the north-east of Market Rasen and can be reached by taking the B1203 from Market Rasen towards Grimsby. On reaching the village of Binbrook, turn left on Orford Road and after half a mile bear right up towards the former entrance. The land is now private but much of the technical, administrative and domestic sites has survived. The former married quarters are now a housing estate and a number of hangars and other buildings can still be seen. The RAF Binbrook Ident Square Memorial, situated on the original wartime 'BK' ident square, is the initiative of former 460 (RAAF) Squadron aircrew and ground personnel and commemorates the station and squadron during the Second World War.

In the village of Binbrook there are other reminders of this airfield's history. On entering the village from the Market Rasen direction, Orford Road bears sharp left towards the airfield and on the right side of that junction is the memorial to 460 (RAAF) squadron. It has the squadron's badge and motto, and was dedicated in 1973. In the village church (St Mary and St Gabriel) there is a stained glass memorial window dedicated in 1989 following the closure of RAF Binbrook to mark the close relationship between the Parish and RAF. The 460 (RAAF) Squadron roll of honour, to commemorate those who were killed during the war, is kept in the chapel. The village of Binbrook fell in love with the Australians, an affinity that has lasted to this day.

Summary of Binbrook during the Second World War

Squadron	Date	Aircraft type
12 Squadron	3 July–6 August 1940	Battle I
	7 September 1940–24 September 1942	Wellington II
142 Squadron	3 July–11 August 1940	Battle I
	6 September 1940–25 November 1941	Wellington II
460 (RAAF) Squadron	14 May 1943–19 July 1945	Lancaster III

CHAPTER TWO

Blyton

Just five miles to the north-east of Gainsborough is the site of the former wartime airfield of Blyton. Although built as an airfield of 1 Group Bomber Command, Blyton saw little service in that role but it still earns its place among Lincolnshire's bomber airfields.

The training of bomber crews was initially carried out at squadron level but with the demand increasing several times over as the war entered its second and then third years, specialist training units were established. Experienced instructors were drawn from the squadrons, either during their operational tour or at the end, with each Bomber Command group assuming responsibility for the training of its crews.

The task for training 1 Group's bomber crews fell on RAF Lindholme in South Yorkshire, but it was never intended for Lindholme to be able to cope with the numbers that required training and so airfields such as Blyton were allocated for the new training units being established to relieve the training burden on Lindholme.

Plans for an airfield at Blyton were initially drawn up in early 1941 and work soon began to construct the airfield on agricultural land just over a mile to the north-east of the village, between Blyton and Northorpe. The airfield was to be built to the standard Class A pattern, with three hardened runways; the main runway of 2,000 yards ran in a north-east to south-west direction, while the two shorter runways, both around 1,400 yards long, ran almost east-west and from the south-east to north-west. A concrete perimeter track linked thirty-six aircraft hard standing dispersals and there were three hangars: a B1 and two T2s, one on the north side and the second on the technical site built to the south-west of the main runway. Accommodation

Part of the former airfield of Blyton is now used as a track for off-road racing cars, called Blyton Park, the entrance of which can be found off the B1205 Kirton Road to the east of the village. (Author)

for the station's personnel and other communal facilities were built on the western side of the airfield along the main road running north from the village of Blyton towards Scunthorpe. Bomb stores were located in surrounding fields and the domestic site was positioned to the north of Blyton village on either side of the A159.

There was no time to waste and just as soon as the runways had been constructed the airfield opened to flying, even before the rest of the technical and domestic facilities had been completed. Blyton was first used as a training base for Polish bomber crews with the first elements of 18 (Polish) Operational Training Unit (OTU), equipped with Vickers Wellingtons, arriving during July 1942. Administrative control of the station was then passed to Hemswell and for two months during the latter half of the year the OTU was joined by 1481 Gunnery Flight (operating a mix of aircraft including the Wellington, Armstrong Whitworth Whitley, Boulton Paul Defiant and the Westland Lysander), which had arrived from Binbrook while its resident airfield was undergoing major development.

But it was not long before the training flight moved out to make way for Blyton's first operational squadron. The airfield had now been officially opened and the new arrivals were the

Wellingtons and crews of 199 Squadron, which re-formed at Blyton in November 1942 as part of 3 Group, an all-Wellington group with squadrons based in eastern England.

The squadron flew its first operational sorties on the night of 6/7 December when six Wellingtons took part in a raid against Mannheim. They were part of a mixed force of 272 aircraft – Lancasters, Halifaxes, Wellingtons and Stirlings – but the bombers arrived to find the target covered in cloud. It was all but impossible for the Pathfinders to lay down markers and so the main stream bomber crews were left to bomb as best they could.

199 Squadron's stay at Blyton was only short-lived. The airfield, with its hardened runways and hard standings, was required for a new HCU being formed and so 199 Squadron moved out to Ingham in February 1943. During its brief stay at Blyton, the squadron had flown more than a hundred sorties and had lost only one aircraft.

With the Wellingtons gone, administrative control of Blyton was passed back to Lindholme once more. Blyton's status was now upgraded from satellite to a sub-station and soon Lancasters, Halifaxes and a few Manchesters started to arrive to form 1662 HCU, a training unit that would remain at Blyton until the end of the war.

Training new crews was never going to be easy. Losses were, at times, as high as those suffered by the front line squadrons during operations and while at Blyton the HCU lost more than fifty aircraft during training sorties. The combination of inexperienced crews and poor weather often proving a recipe for disaster.

With losses mounting on the operational Lancaster squadrons, particularly during the costly campaign against Berlin in the winter of 1943/44, the decision was made to form the Lancaster Finishing School (LFS) to help new crews cope better with the training gap between the HCUs, usually completed on aircraft such as the Halifax, and the front-line squadrons. The LFS was initially intended to be based at Blyton but was eventually set up at Hemswell. As this meant pooling all available Lancaster training resources at Hemswell, the Lancasters of 1662 HCU left to form part of the LFS, leaving at Blyton only the thirty or so Halifaxes still on the HCU's strength at that time.

Although the runway and hard standings had been built with the operation of heavy bombers in mind, Blyton, being a training base, was never afforded any further priority and so any damage to the operating surfaces never seemed to be fully repaired. Facilities were rarely completed and it also seems that it was never intended for Blyton to accommodate so many people. And so for the 1,500-plus service men and women based there at its peak during the summer of 1944, during which as many as forty bomber crews were being trained at any one time, conditions were makeshift at best. As such, crews were seemingly quite happy to finally arrive at their operational units after their time training with the HCU.

By the end of 1944 Blyton had been passed to 7 (Training) Group, along with 1 Group's other training units, with the new group responsible for the training of all Bomber Command crews. But by early 1945 there were more than enough bomber crews to fill the front line and so this led to a drawdown in training at Blyton as the war approached its final phase.

With its training role no longer required, 1662 HCU disbanded in April 1945. Blyton then became home to one of the RAF's Aircrew Holding Units and during the months following the end of the war several thousand aircrew passed through Blyton as part of the demob process. The airfield then closed to flying and was put on care and maintenance, although it briefly re-opened during the 1950s when Blyton was used as a relief landing ground for the flying training school at nearby RAF Finningley.

In spite of ideas to refurbish Blyton for use by the Americans during the early years of the Cold War, the airfield was never used again. By the early 1960s the land had been sold off, mostly for agricultural use. The runways were dug up and the hangars sold, although some of the brick buildings and parts of the perimeter track remained. Part of the former airfield is now used for off-road racing cars, called Blyton Park.

The site of the former airfield can be reached by taking the A159 from Gainsborough towards Scunthorpe. Having passed through the village of Blyton, the A159 marks the western boundary of the former airfield, with a minor road running eastwards, called Dring Lane, marking the extent of the northern part of the former airfield. The B1205 Kirton Road, which runs east from the village, marks the airfield's southern boundary. On leaving the village of Blyton, the southern threshold of the former main runway is about half a mile along the B1205. The entrance to Blyton Park can be found just before the road takes a sharp left. The racing track marks the eastern part of the former airfield and marks the threshold of the runway that once ran from the east to the west.

Summary of Blyton during the Second World War

Squadron	Date	Aircraft type
199 Squadron	7 November 1942–2 February 1943	Wellington III

CHAPTER THREE

Elsham Wolds

Ten miles to the north-east of Scunthorpe is the site of the former airfield of Elsham Wolds. First used as an aerodrome by the Home Defence squadrons of the Royal Flying Corps, this airfield has a long history. But with the First World War over, the airfield was closed and for a while the land reverted to agriculture before Elsham was brought alive once more following the outbreak of the Second World War.

Work began on the former site in 1940 and in July 1941 Elsham Wolds re-opened as part of 1 Group Bomber Command, and one of the first of Lincolnshire's new bomber airfields of the war. Within days of the airfield opening, Wellingtons of 103 Squadron arrived and Elsham would remain the squadron's home for the rest of the war.

The airfield had been constructed with three standard hardened runways but in those early days the rest of the facilities were basic and incomplete, and it would be several weeks before the airfield was considered suitable for more personnel. Elsham was then under the command of Group Captain Hugh Constantine, a former Wellington squadron commander and a man who would become a pivotal character within Bomber Command. He would later work closely with the aeronautical engineer Barnes Wallis in the development of newer and heavier weapons for the bombing of key industrial and hardened targets of Nazi Germany, and after the war he would go on to reach the rank of air chief marshal.

103 Squadron was soon taking part in operations from its new home. Just a few days after arriving at Elsham its Wellingtons helped make up a force of nearly a hundred aircraft detailed to attack the German port of Bremen on the night of 14/15 July. Then, the following week, on 24 July, the squadron suffered

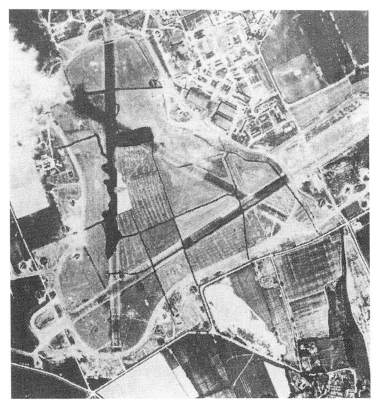

A classic airborne wartime picture of Elsham Wolds showing the effort made to disrupt and blend the pattern of the airfield into the surrounding countryside through the use of paint and other materials. (Author's collection via Ken Delve)

its first loss when one of its aircraft, flown by Sergeant John Bucknole, failed to return from a daylight raid against German warships at Brest. No fighter escort was available for the raid and so the Wellington crews were left to press on alone against the heavily defended ships. The battleship *Gneisenau*, which was undergoing repairs in dock at the time, was claimed as being hit a number of times and it is believed that Bucknole and his crew were lost during these attacks.

One notable young pilot to arrive at Elsham during October 1941 was Flight Lieutenant David Holford. Although he was still only twenty years old, Holford already wore the ribbon of a DFC having completed a tour of operations as a Wellington pilot. He had joined the RAF at the age of seventeen, was an aircraft captain at the age of nineteen and had been awarded his DFC at the same age. He had then served as an instructor before arriving at Elsham for his second operational tour. Holford flew twenty-nine ops with 103 Squadron, one of them being against the mighty German warships – *Scharnhorst, Gneisenau* and *Prinz Eugen* – during their daring daylight dash through the English Channel on 12 February 1942.

The ships were attempting to reach the North Sea and then the safety of a German port but bad weather and poor visibility had meant the RAF and the Royal Navy had been caught unaware that the ships were even in the Channel. There was little time to react and so the British had only managed to get a small number of aircraft airborne in time to mount any attacks. One aircraft to carry out an attack was a Wellington flown by Holford. He was flying with another squadron aircraft flown by his flight commander, 23-year-old Squadron Leader Ian Cross. They had been the only squadron pilots available after an earlier call had stood down other crews because of the bad weather. Both Wellingtons bravely attacked the heavily defended warships, Holford managing to put his bombs close to the ships. However, his aircraft had been hit many times by the ferocious barrage of anti-aircraft fire put up by the ships, although not enough to bring the aircraft down. Cross, though, was not so lucky. His aircraft was shot down, although the crew survived and were picked up to become prisoners of war. But despite surviving that day, Ian Cross would not survive the war. He was one of fifty airmen executed in March 1944 after being captured during what later became known as the Great Escape.

Although the German warships had escaped relatively unscathed, David Holford was awarded the DSO for his perseverance and courage during the attack, after which he was promoted to the rank of squadron leader. The squadron then converted to the Halifax, the only squadron in 1 Group to be so equipped, with Holford selected to lead the squadron's heavy conversion flight. He then led the squadron's first operations with the new type during a raid against Düsseldorf at the end of July.

The memorial to RAF Elsham Wolds, showing the plaques of 103 and 576 Squadrons, which operated from the airfield during the Second World War, can be found outside the Anglian Water Authority on Middlegate Lane, which has been built on the western edge of the former airfield. (Author)

Holford was still only twenty-one years old and once his tour with the squadron was over he left for another instructional tour, but he would sadly be killed later in the war while leading 100 Squadron at Grimsby (see Grimsby for more about Holford). At the time of his death he was the RAF's youngest wing commander at the age of just twenty-two.

In November 1942, and after just four months of operating the Halifax, 103 Squadron became the first of 1 Group's squadrons to be equipped with the Lancaster. The arrival of the Lancaster also meant that 103 became the only squadron within the group to operate all four types of aircraft during the war: the Battle, Wellington, Halifax and Lancaster. For the squadron's crews, the Lancaster was also seen to have arrived just in time as losses with the Halifax had been high.

The squadron's first operations with the Lancaster, a minelaying sortie in the Bay of Biscay, was carried out by six squadron aircraft on the night of 21/22 November; all aircraft returned safely. The arrival of the Lancaster marked a new phase for Elsham Wolds and one notable aircraft to have operated from the airfield was to become one of the RAF's legendary Lancs. ED888, with the squadron code 'PM-M Mother', was delivered to 103 Squadron in April 1943 and flew its first op early the following month against Dortmund. The aircraft soon became the trusted mount of Sergeant (later Pilot Officer) Denis Rudge who flew the aircraft on its second op and went on to complete twenty-five missions in 'M-Mother' during his successful tour of operations, which ended in September 1943.

At the end of November ED888 was transferred to a new squadron being formed at Elsham. This was 576 Squadron, formed from C Flight of 103 Squadron, and so ED888 now became 'UL-V Victor'. The new squadron commenced operations on the night of 2/3 December. Its first target was Berlin, known to the crews as the Big City, during the early days of what would later become known as the Battle of Berlin.

The re-organization of Bomber Command saw Elsham assume control of the satellite airfields at Kirmington and North Killingholme. This meant the erection of more hangars and buildings at Elsham, plus the arrival of more station personnel, to cope with the additional workload. During its peak, when some 2,500 personnel were based at Elsham, its squadrons were sending up to forty aircraft a night on operations, with 103 Squadron holding an unofficial record for sending thirty aircraft on a single operation during the height of the bombing offensive against Berlin.

It was at the end of this hard campaign in March 1944 that ED888 was re-designated 'UL-M Mike' with a small number '2' next to the aircraft's individual code-letter 'M', and so ED888 simply became known as 'Mike-Squared'. The aircraft then became the regular mount of Pilot Officer Jimmy Griffiths and his crew who flew 'Mike-Squared' on all but two of their thirty ops. One of their ops in 'Mike-Squared' was the costly attack against a German military camp at Mailly-le-Camp on the night of 3/4 May, a raid carried out by 346 Lancasters from 1 and 5 Groups, when forty-two aircraft were lost. Although 'Mike-Squared' was one to make it safely back home, seven of Elsham's aircraft had failed to return.

For Jimmy Griffiths and his crew their tour of operations came to an end in July 1944, after which 'Mike-Squared' was taken over by the crew of Pilot Officer James Bell. Bell had flown as second pilot to Griffiths on the crew's final op against Revigny on the night of 14/15 July, another costly night for Elsham when another seven aircraft failed to return, after which Bell then flew the aircraft with his own crew on their first operation on 20 July. It was the milestone 100th op for 'Mike-Squared' and the target was the V-weapon storage site at Wizernes. Fortunately, the reliable and trusted 'Mike-Squared' came through unscathed and it was the start of another close relationship between aircraft and crew. Bell's crew went on to complete their tour of thirty straight ops in the aircraft. Not once was it used by another crew on ops during this time, with Bell's crew successfully completing their tour in October 1944.

It was at that same time, October 1944, when 576 Squadron left Elsham Wolds, leaving 103 as the airfield's only resident squadron until the final days of the war. For the record, 'Mike-Squared' remained at Elsham having been transferred back to 103 Squadron following the departure of 576. The legendary ED888 now became 'PM-M2'. It had already flown a staggering 131 missions and went on to complete another nine before 'Mike-Squared' was retired from ops in January 1945, having completed nearly a thousand hours of operational flying.

With hostilities in Europe coming to an end, 100 Squadron re-formed at Elsham Wolds and its Lancasters flew from the airfield during the final days of the war, although the squadron had moved out again before the end of the year. The end of 1945 also saw the disbandment of 103 Squadron, Elsham's longest serving residents. The squadron is credited with having flown more operational sorties than any other 1 Group squadron during the war. However, with this record came the group's highest losses with nearly 200 of the 248 aircraft lost from Elsham having belonged to the squadron.

With the departure of the last operational squadron, the airfield then became home to a mix of aircraft – Halifaxes, Albermarles and Horsa gliders – until the end of 1946, by which time they had all moved out and the airfield closed.

The site of the former airfield can be found just over a mile to the north of the village of Elsham and can be reached by taking the M180 eastbound towards Grimsby. At the last junction of the motorway, take the first exit off the roundabout towards Elsham village. Having passed through the village, turn right on to the B1206 and about a mile up the hill is a three-way junction, where Middlegate Lane and Wold Road meet the B1206. To the east

In the entrance to the main foyer of the Anglian Water Authority building is a lasting tribute to all those who served at Elsham Wolds during the Second World War. (Author)

of this junction is the former airfield. The line of Wold Road marks the northern extremity while turning right at the three-way junction and following Middlegate Lane south-eastwards marks the western edge. Along Middlegate Lane is the Anglian Water Authority, which has been built on the edge of the former airfield at the end of one of its runways. In the entrance foyer to the main building is a memorial plaque. It was dedicated in 1975 and displays the badges of 1 Group and 103 Squadron. Also on display in the foyer are a number of boards commemorating those who served at the airfield during the Second World War, while outside the building there is a memorial garden with two propeller blades and central hub, and a memorial stone dedicated to 103 and 576 Squadrons.

The eastern part of the former airfield is now an industrial estate, which can be found by continuing northbound from the M180 along the A15 towards the Humber Bridge (instead of turning towards the village of Elsham) for just over a mile. Several roads on the industrial estate have RAF-related names, such as Halifax Approach and Merlin Drive. The northerly end of the estate marks the area where one of the runways, the north-east to south-west runway, crossed what is now the A15 link road to the Humber Bridge.

Summary of Elsham Wolds during the Second World War

Squadron	Date	Aircraft type
103 Squadron	11 July 1941–26 November 1945	Wellington/Halifax/Lancaster
576 Squadron	25 November 1943–30 October 1944	Lancaster I/III
100 Squadron	1 April–2 December 1945	Lancaster I/III

CHAPTER FOUR

Faldingworth

Just five miles or so to the south-west of Market Rasen is the site of the former wartime airfield of Faldingworth, one of the later Bomber Command airfields to have been completed during the Second World War and best remembered for its close association with the Polish airmen of 300 (Mazowiecki) Squadron, a friendship that has lasted to this day.

The site was first used as a decoy airfield during the early years of the war, with wooden Whitley bombers scattered over a field. But with Bomber Command expanding its number of squadrons and an increased requirement for more airfields, the land was soon selected for further development and a standard pattern bomber airfield was constructed.

The airfield of Faldingworth was allocated to 1 Group as a satellite training base for Lindholme in South Yorkshire. Although still some way short of being completed, Faldingworth opened in the summer of 1943 under the command of Group Captain Neil Mason. The first aircraft to arrive were Halifaxes and Lancasters of 1667 HCU, although the Lancasters soon moved out to Hemswell as part of the LFS. It would still be some time before work was completed at the airfield and so for a while Faldingworth operated just Halifaxes in the training role, and it was not until early 1944 that the airfield was ready to accommodate an operational squadron.

Faldingworth was now part of 14 Base headquartered at Ludford Magna and by the end of February 1944 the HCU had moved out to make way for the arrival of the Wellingtons of 300 (Mazowiecki) Squadron. This Polish squadron was one of a number of overseas squadrons made up of personnel who had fled their occupied homeland to continue the fight against Nazi Germany, with the low 300-series of squadron number plates

Squadron Leader Ludwik Kurowski and the crew of 300 (Mazowiecki) Squadron pictured at Faldingworth in front of Lancaster 'BH-C' in April 1944. This Polish crew were lost just days later when they failed to return from a raid against Karlsruhe on the night of 24/25 April 1944. (Faldingworth Memorial Group via Colin Mitchell-Smith)

allocated to the Poles. With most of the squadron's aircrew being Poles, there was an understandable feeling of aggression and a need for revenge against Europe's Nazi occupiers. Some of the pilots had already flown in combat, either when serving with the Polish Air Force at the time Germany invaded their country, or since making their way to Britain.

The Poles flew their first operations from Faldingworth on the night of 3/4 March 1944. These were minelaying sorties with three aircraft laying mines in the approaches to the U-boat base at Lorient on the Atlantic coast of north-west France. All three aircraft returned safely and it effectively brought to an end Bomber Command's operational use of the Wellington.

Lancasters now started to arrive at Faldingworth and the Poles flew their first operational sorties with the new type on the night of 18/19 April when aircraft of 300 (Mazowiecki) Squadron joined a raiding force of 273 Lancasters, mostly from 1 Group, to carry out an attack against railway marshalling yards at the French city of Rouen. Bomber Command was now supporting the build-up to the Allied landings in north-west Europe and so the destruction of railway yards in northern France would severely disrupt the enemy's troop movements and later prevent reinforcements from reaching the battlefield. Not only was the raid reported to be a success, with much destruction caused to the yards, all aircraft returned safely.

Station personnel at Faldingworth pulled out all the stops to ensure the Poles were always present when it came to bombing the enemy, and the squadron quickly earned respect within the hierarchy of Bomber Command during this very busy period of operations.

For the latter half of 1944 the airfield was also home to Oxfords of 1546 Beam Approach Training Flight (BATF) but the Poles of 300 remained the only resident squadron at Faldingworth until the end of the war, by which time they had taken part in the majority of Bomber Command's Main Force efforts; the last raid from the airfield was the attack against Hitler's Eagle's Nest and the local SS barracks at Berchtesgaden on 25 April 1945.

With hostilities over the Poles remained at Faldingworth until 300 (Mazowiecki) Squadron was finally disbanded at the end of 1946. It had briefly been joined during its final days by Mosquitos of another Polish unit, 305 (Weilkopolski) Squadron, which had returned to the UK to disband after serving with the Allied occupying forces in Europe. Faldingworth had unusually been designated a Polish Air Force base for part of this time, and not an RAF station.

With the disbandment of both Polish squadrons, the airfield was then closed to flying and was placed on care and maintenance. Although Faldingworth never returned to its flying status, the airfield was used as a nuclear weapons storage site from the late 1950s until 1972 when the airfield closed down. Part of the former airfield was then used by the British Manufacture and Research Company for armament development and demonstration, after which it was used by the Royal Ordnance factory. The site is now used by Skydock, which offers widespread testing services and solutions and manages the Faldingworth range, the most advanced of its type in the world.

The former airfield can be found to the west of the village of Faldingworth and can be reached by taking the A46 towards Market Rasen. On entering the village of Faldingworth turn left into Spridlington Road towards the village of Spridlington and after about two miles the road marks the southern boundary

A memorial to all those who served with 300 (Mazowiecki) Squadron and 1667 Heavy Conversion Unit during 1943–47 stands at the eastern end of what remains of the former main runway at Faldingworth. (Author)

of the former airfield with the Skydock site marking the south-western corner; the small village of Newtoft marks the north-eastern corner.

In 2004 an airfield memorial was erected at the eastern end of what remains of the former runway, which ran almost east–west, and dedicated to all those who served with 300 (Mazowiecki) Squadron and 1667 HCU during 1943–47. The memorial is constructed from concrete blocks broken from the old runway, perimeter track, aircraft standings and buildings; these represent the broken lives and tragedy of war. Inside the base are placed small parts from some of the aircraft lost while flying from the airfield. Out of the base rises three columns of stone that came from the Lincoln Cathedral quarry; the cathedral was a welcome sight when returning from operations. Behind the memorial is the old windsock, now used as a flag pole. The memorial can only be visited with prior permission as access to the site is restricted.

In the village church (All Saints), which can be found on the left side of the High Street when passing through Faldingworth towards Market Rasen, there is a memorial plaque mounted on the wall of the north side of the church. The plaque depicts the ensign of the Polish Air Force and is dedicated to the Polish men and women who served at Faldingworth during the period

The lasting connection between Faldingworth and the Poles of 300 (Mazowiecki) Squadron is evident in the village church (All Saints), which includes a stained glass window. Under the window is a small cabinet containing photos and reminders of the former airfield. (Author)

1944–47. Next to the plaque is a stained glass window dedicated to 300 (Mazowiecki) Squadron. At the base of the window is the Polish Air Force chequerboard and the RAF roundel, under which a small cabinet contains photos and reminders of the former airfield. The gates into the church, constructed in hand-forged steel, commemorate the sacrifices made by the Poles of 300 (Mazowiecki) Squadron and commemorate the coming together of peoples to join in a common cause. Leading up to the church is the Path of Friendship, paved with slabs and with brick edgings in the Polish colours of red and white on the north and east side (facing Poland) and, on the opposite side, are the British colours of red, white and blue. The colours tie into two hands, symbolically shaking in friendship, at the porch gate. Please note the church is kept locked out of service hours.

Summary of Faldingworth during the Second World War

Squadron	Date	Aircraft type
300 (Mazowiecki) Squadron	1 March 1944–2 January 1947	Wellington/ Lancaster I/III

CHAPTER FIVE

Grimsby (Waltham)

F ive miles to the south of Grimsby is the former wartime airfield of the same name, although the airfield is often referred to as Waltham after the village next to where it was built. As far as its official name is concerned, the airfield was called RAF Grimsby (Waltham) during the early years of the Second World War but the title changed during Bomber Command's reorganization of 1943 and was shortened to RAF Grimsby.

Compared with some of the more remote Bomber Command airfields in Lincolnshire, the airfield, with its close proximity to the town of Grimsby and the coast, seems to have been a popular posting during the Second World War. The airfield had first been used as a civilian landing ground during the late 1930s but it was also home to one of the RAF's elementary flying training schools during 1938. At that time the airfield was known as Grimsby Municipal Airport, one of a number of small airports around the country used to operate internal domestic flights, although flying around the UK was not a particularly popular or profitable venture at the time.

In truth, the Second World War probably saved the site. With France having fallen in June 1940, this pre-war airfield was requisitioned by the Air Ministry for development as a bomber airfield. Although it was all grass at the time, the site was one of many considered suitable for 1 Group but rather than rush the airfield into service, it was decided to spend time and money to make it suitable for the operation of heavy bombers all year round.

Work took eighteen months to complete, including the construction of hardened runways and hard standings, and, in November 1941, Grimsby officially opened as a satellite of

The former airfield of Grimsby pictured some fifty years after the Second World War and clearly shows its close proximity to the village of Holton-le-Clay with the main A16 separating the two. (via the Lincolnshire Echo)

Binbrook. At that time Binbrook was home to two Wellington squadrons and one of these, 142 Squadron, became the first resident unit at Grimsby. The squadron personnel had no time to settle in as the Wellingtons were required to continue the night war against targets in Germany.

With the exception of just a month, when the squadron was briefly moved south, 142 remained at Grimsby until the end of 1942 when it moved out in preparation for a move overseas to be replaced by 100 Squadron, which re-formed at Grimsby as a heavy bomber squadron. But it would be a few weeks before the first Lancasters were due to arrive as the airfield needed to be improved before operations with the larger and heavier Lancaster could commence; the runway had to be extended and other changes to the technical site had to be made.

The first of the squadron's initial establishment of sixteen Lancasters arrived during January 1943. Because of ongoing work the squadron's operational work-up was carried out mostly at other airfields but by the beginning of March it was considered ready to join Bomber Command's Main Force.

100 Squadron carried out its first operational sorties from Grimsby on the night of 4/5 March 1943. There was no major effort that night and so the Lancasters went off on a minelaying sortie around the French Atlantic port of St Nazaire. One aircraft was lost in the area while another had to make a forced landing at another airfield in Nottinghamshire on its way home. It had not been a great start but four nights later the squadron took part in its first major bombing effort of the war when it formed part of a mixed force of 335 bombers – Lancasters, Halifaxes and Stirlings – detailed to attack Nuremberg. Although the crews arrived overhead the target to find it clear of cloud, there was no moon that night and a layer of haze over the city prevented visual identification of the target, causing bombing to be spread over a large area.

It was the start of what was to be later called the Battle of the Ruhr. The squadron was commanded during this period by Wing Commander R V McIntyre who was awarded the DFC for bringing a damaged Lancaster back to England following a raid against Bochum on the night of 13/14 May. His aircraft had been hit by flak while overhead Cologne, taking out two of his engines, but McIntyre pressed on to Bochum to complete his attack before heading for home. He eventually managed to make a crash-landing at Coltishall in Norfolk.

As a satellite airfield of Binbrook, Grimsby had been under the overall command of Group Captain Hughie Edwards (see Binbrook for more about Edwards), but following the re-organization of Bomber Command's airfields in 1943, Grimsby became an airfield in its own right. Commanded by Group Captain 'Nick' Carter, Grimsby became part of 12 Base with its headquarters at Binbrook and under the overall command of the legendary Air Commodore Arthur Wray (see Binbrook and Hemswell for more about Wray).

The Battle of the Ruhr lasted for more than four months. In just eight raids during June 1943, 100 Squadron lost nine Lancasters – one-third of its strength at the time. The campaign over the Ruhr was followed by the Battle of Hamburg and then the Battle of Berlin, which was conducted during the winter of 1943/44. The squadron's first raid against Berlin took place on the night of 18/19 November. With 440 Lancasters taking part that night,

The former airfield of Grimsby can be accessed today by public footpaths running through the site. This is the north-eastern part of the former airfield where an old wartime hangar has survived, as have parts of the runway and perimeter track. (Author)

it marked the opening of a long and costly campaign against the Big City.

Two days later saw the arrival at Grimsby of Wing Commander David Holford. With McIntyre's tour of duty having come to an end, the remarkably young Holford arrived to take command of the squadron. Seeing such a young and fresh-faced 22-year-old wing commander would, no doubt, have turned heads at Grimsby. But closer inspection of his battle tunic – showing the ribbons of the DSO and DFC – would have instantly proved to any potential doubters that Holford had earned his command.

David Holford had become Bomber Command's youngest wing commander when promoted to the rank four days before his twenty-second birthday. By then he had already completed two tours of operations (see Elsham Wolds for more about Holford). But the gallant Holford's life was soon to end following a raid against Berlin on the night of 16/17 December. Like so many other tragic stories of the loss of airmen during the Second World War, it was Holford's eagerness and courage that was to ultimately cost him his life as he need not have been in action that night. He had put himself on to the battle order that morning to help a crew that had been going through a particularly bad time.

Because of the distance to the target and the time of year, take-off was early at around 4.30 pm. It was to be a long round-trip of some eight hours or more, and as the crews climbed out over the North Sea it immediately became apparent that weather conditions were far from ideal for the raid. The forecast had been for upper level cloud to offer the bomber crews some protection but visibility was found to be clear once the crews had climbed above the medium level cloud. There was, however, some hope as fog had been forecast over north-west Europe, and this would hopefully keep the Luftwaffe's night fighters on the ground. But this did not prove to be the case. During the long transit to Belin Holford's aircraft was attacked by a night fighter but, although the Lancaster suffered damage, he pressed on. His aircraft had, however, fallen behind the main bomber stream but he continued to Berlin and successfully bombed the target. Then, on the way home, his Lancaster was attacked again but despite the damage to his aircraft, Holford managed to get it back to a position overhead Grimsby where he found the base to be covered by low cloud and fog.

It was not just Grimsby that was covered by low cloud and fog. So, too, was all of North Lincolnshire. Several aircraft were holding over the coast trying to find a place to land and so Holford decided to hold off and wait until the less experienced crews had been given the chance to get down.

With his own aircraft running desperately short of fuel, Holford eventually attempted a landing at Kelstern in poor visibility but the tail of his aircraft clipped rising ground, causing the rear turret to break away and the aircraft to crash. Three of the crew were killed but the impact had thrown others clear of the wreckage. The wireless operator, Sergeant Eric MacKay, had survived and stumbling around in the darkness he came across Holford lying in the snow on the ground. His legs were broken and there were some visible signs of injuries on his forehead but at that stage Holford was still alive. He was even muttering words of concern about whether the crew were all right. It was a bitterly cold night and so MacKay wrapped Holford in a parachute but help was a long time coming. The number of crashes and incidents had stretched the rescue crews to the limit and by the time help arrived, the gallant David Holford was dead.

It had been a bad night for the squadron and for Grimsby. In addition to the loss of Holford's Lancaster, two other Grimsby aircraft had collided over the airfield and another had crashed just a mile or so away near the village of Barnoldby le Beck; all twenty-one crew members of these three aircraft were killed. The only positive outcome from the night was an inquiry into the losses, which led to the introduction of an initiative known as the 'Waltham Circle' where local searchlights were used to help guide the bombers back to their base in bad weather.

The night of 16/17 December 1943 was also a disastrous night for Bomber Command and was later dubbed 'Black Thursday'. Twenty-five Lancasters failed to return from the actual raid on Berlin but a further twenty-nine were lost having returned to England only to encounter poor weather at their bases, either by crashing while attempting to land or having been abandoned when the crews were faced with no option other than to bale out.

Black Thursday also involved another Grimsby-based squadron as for a brief period at the end of 1943, 100 Squadron was not operating alone from the airfield. This other unit was 550 Squadron, which had been formed at the end of November using the nucleus of 100 Squadron's C Flight. Commanded by Wing Commander Jimmy Bennett, 550 had begun operations immediately and so had taken part in the raid against Berlin that night. Bennett and his crew were among the lucky ones to have survived Black Thursday. Bennett had descended below the cloud over the North Sea rather than to try and get down through it over Lincolnshire and had arrived at Grimsby before the worst of the fog, and so he managed to get down safely.

It had never been intended for Grimsby to accommodate two heavy bomber squadrons and so 550 soon moved to North Killingholme, arriving there in the first few days of 1944, to leave just 100 Squadron at Grimsby until the final days of the war. Sadly though, Holford's replacement, Wing Commander John Dilworth, was also to die in action. He was killed during a raid against Schweinfurt on the night of 24/25 February 1944.

Dilworth's loss marked the end of a hard first year for 100 Squadron at Grimsby. But the squadron had played its part in the relentless night war over occupied Europe, having taken part in every major raid in the strategic bombing campaign against

Nazi Germany. The squadron had flown the second highest number of 1 Group bombing sorties but done remarkably well to have suffered the fewest losses.

The base commander, Air Commodore Arthur Wray, had been a regular visitor during the hard winter of 1943/44 and he flew his last operational sortie from Grimsby on the night of 15/16 March 1944 at the age of forty-seven. He was an inspiration to all his crews as later recounted by Douglas Sutton, then a young sergeant pilot with only seven hours of flying time on the Lancaster, who flew with Wray that night.

Sutton and his brand new crew, all young sergeants and around twenty years old, had only arrived at Grimsby the week before. On the morning of their first op Sutton was told that his crew were to fly that night with the base commander! The sprog crew had never seen such a senior officer before and watching the stocky and grey-haired figure of Arthur Wray limping out towards the Lancaster made an unforgettable sight. But Wray's unparalleled reputation and array of medal ribbons, combined with his naturally warm smile and relaxed manner, soon put the young crew at ease. In Sutton's own words they 'took to him at once'.

Flying in 'HW-J Jig', they were one of more than 600 Lancasters of a total force of more than 850 aircraft detailed to attack Stuttgart, one of Germany's most viciously defended targets. They soon became separated from the main bomber stream and with the threat of night fighters and their radar now being jammed, the crew might well have chosen to turn around and return to Grimsby. But Wray would not entertain the idea. His experience and calmness enabled the crew to plot an approximate course to the target.

Having arrived over Stuttgart slightly late and still alone, Wray began the bombing run through heavy flak. Stuttgart's defences were wide awake and from the bombers that had gone through before, the anti-aircraft gunners were fully aware of the height and direction of attack. It was, therefore, a difficult run-in to the target and not satisfied with their approach, Wray coolly decided to go around again, a difficult decision for the most experienced crew to take let alone for one on their first op. But Wray was keen to impress on the young crew the importance of accuracy and having circled overhead the city they started their second run through the flak. Then, with their bombs finally gone, they turned away to start the long journey home. Even then Wray had not stopped teaching the young crew and so he demonstrated the gut-wrenching 'corkscrew' manoeuvre, an evasive technique that might just save the crew one day. Having returned safely to Grimsby after eight hours in the air, Sutton was later reported to have said that 'Air Commodore Wray was the most remarkable man I had ever known' and that the time spent circling overhead Stuttgart 'seemed interminable but Wray set an example in the heat of the action which no training school could hope to match'.

With the hard winter of 1943/44 over, Bomber Command turned its attention to supporting the Allied landings of north-west Europe. Like many other bomber units, 100 Squadron was in action on D-Day, bombing coastal batteries in support of the Allied landings, and was then involved with attacking a variety of targets to support the breakout from the Normandy beachhead during the following days and weeks.

The squadron had many great aircraft on its books during its time at Grimsby, one of which was EE139, later to become known as the 'Phantom of the Ruhr', which flew the first thirty-two of its eventual total of 121 ops with 100 Squadron. It had joined the squadron in May 1943 and only left in November because it was one of the aircraft transferred to 550 Squadron when it formed at Grimsby, after which the squadron and EE139 moved to North Killingholme.

But 100 Squadron's three most notable Lancasters, all of which were centurions, were JB603, ND458 and ND644. With overall losses reducing during the latter months of the war, it allowed some airframes to mount up impressive totals but, sadly, two of these, would not see out hostilities. The first, JB603, failed to return from a raid against Hannover on the night of 5/6 January 1945 with all but one of Flying Officer Reg Barker's crew killed; it was the aircraft's 111th sortie. The second, ND644, known on the squadron as 'N-Nan', flew 128 ops (although sources vary) but failed to return from a raid against Nuremberg on the night of 16/17 March 1945. The aircraft was captained by 24-year-old Flying Officer George Dauphinee and all but two of his mainly Canadian crew were killed. However, ND458, the third of the squadron's centurions and probably the most famous,

The memorial to 100 Squadron stands on the edge of the former airfield of Grimsby and can be found on the A16 near the traffic lights at the turn-off to the village to Holton-le-Clay. (Author)

did survive the war. Affectionately known on the squadron as 'Able Mable', this legendary Lanc flew 134 ops (including its last seven sorties on Operations *Exodus* and *Manna*).

By the time 'Able Mable' flew its last bombing sortie of the war, against the SS barracks at Berchtesgaden on 25 April 1945, 100 Squadron had left Grimsby to fly its final sorties of the war from Elsham Wolds. During its time operating from Grimsby, 100 Squadron dropped more than 18,000 tons of bombs in nearly 4,000 sorties, although more than a hundred Lancasters had failed to return with the loss of nearly 600 lives.

With the departure of 100 Squadron, Grimsby soon closed to flying. Although ideas about its future were discussed, the airfield never reverted to its pre-war status as a municipal airport and the site soon fell into general disrepair and later reverted to agriculture.

The former airfield can be found on the western side of the A16 just to the south-east of the village of Waltham and to the west of Holton-le-Clay. A memorial stone to 100 Squadron, dedicated in 1978, can be found on the western side of the A16 Holton-le-Clay bypass, at its northern end and near the traffic lights at the turn-off to the village. This area marks the north-eastern part of the former airfield and a former hangar, now used for

agricultural purposes, can still be seen. A walk along the public
footpaths takes you onto the former airfield. The runway that
was aligned in almost a north–south direction ran parallel by a
hundred metres or so to where the A16 runs today. The Tollbar
Academy (then the Waltham Toll Bar School) provides an idea
today where the Lancasters would have been just about to touch
down when using the southerly runway. The Waltham Windmill
Golf Club marks the western side of the former airfield and an
imaginary point on the A16, around 400 metres to the south of
the memorial, marks where the north-east to south-west aligned
runway once was.

Summary of Grimsby during the Second World War

Squadron	Date	Aircraft type
142 Squadron	26 November 1941–6 June 1942	Wellington IV
	7 July–18 December 1942	Wellington III/IV
100 Squadron	15 December 1942–31 March 1945	Lancaster I/III
550 Squadron	25 November 1943–2 January 1944	Lancaster I/III

CHAPTER SIX

Hemswell

Thirteen miles to the north of Lincoln, and just to the north of the village of Harpswell, is the site of Hemswell airfield, which, today, receives thousands of visitors each year to its antiques centre and Sunday market. This airfield could easily be included under those of 5 Group, for it was part of that group at the start of the Second World War, but is included here as it was under 1 Group that Hemswell spent most of its wartime days.

Originally called Harpswell, the site had first been used by the Royal Flying Corps during the First World War. As with many former aerodromes, the land was assessed as suitable for development during the RAF's expansion scheme of the mid-1930s and, in 1936, the new airfield of Hemswell opened as part of 3 Group Bomber Command.

By the outbreak of the Second World War Hemswell had been transferred to 5 Group. The airfield was then under the command of Group Captain Edgar Rice, later to command 1 Group, and home to two squadrons of Hampdens: 144 and 61 Squadrons.

Unlike many other new bomber airfields, Hemswell was ready to commence operations straight away – it was the only airfield in northern Lincolnshire ready to do so – and so its two Hampden squadrons were involved in Bomber Command's early operations of the war; the first ops from Hemswell were reconnaissance missions flown on 26 September 1939.

Three days later, twelve Hampdens of 144 Squadron crossed the North Sea to attack enemy warships heading for the German port of Wilhelmshaven. Led by its squadron commander, 31-year-old Wing Commander Jim Cunningham, it was to be the squadron's first opportunity to hit the enemy. With each aircraft

Wellingtons of 300 (Mazowiecki) Squadron pictured at Hemswell. The Polish squadron spent nearly a year at the airfield during 1941–42. (Author's collection via Ken Delve)

armed with four 500 lb bombs, the Hampdens headed across the North Sea in two sections but the excitement and optimism amongst the crews soon disappeared. Not only did they arrive to find the German warships defended by a wall of anti-aircraft flak, Luftwaffe fighters from an airfield in northern Germany were providing additional cover from above. The Hampdens stood no chance. Five were shot down and amongst those killed was Cunningham. It had been a disastrous start to Hemswell's war.

For the early months of the war RAF bomber crews had not been permitted to drop bombs on German soil but that changed in March 1940 and amongst the first to drop bombs on a German target, in what was the biggest raid of the war so far, were Hampdens of 61 Squadron. The attack took place on the night of 19/20 March against a German seaplane base at Hörnum on the southern tip of the island of Sylt. The Hampdens were part of an attacking force of fifty aircraft and it was several days before the outcome of the raid was known. Damage was minimal but the raid had marked a significant event in the early phase of the war.

For the next month Hemswell's two squadrons took part in minelaying operations in the approaches and surrounds of the

German port at Wilhelmshaven. Then, in July, the Hampdens were given another opportunity to hit the German warships when the two squadrons carried out a daring attack against the *Tirpitz* and *Admiral Scheer*. Once again it was a costly attack, as it would always be against the mighty German warships, with no damage to the ships observed and four Hampdens lost from the attacking force of fifteen.

The two Hemswell squadrons struggled on with great courage for another year but the truth was that the Hampden was barely suitable for the task the crews were being given and so losses were high. In July 1941 the Hampdens moved out and it was at that point that Hemswell was transferred to 1 Group, with two Polish Wellington squadrons, 300 (Mazowiecki) and 301 (Pomorski) Squadrons, moving in.

Many of the young and inexperienced Polish crews were to benefit from the arrival of the new station commander, Group Captain Arthur Wray, who took over command of Hemswell in November 1941. Affectionately known to those who served under him as 'Father', because of his age (he was forty-five) and background as a Royal Flying Corps pilot during the First World War, Wray had already flown on an op to Cologne earlier in the year but was about to embark on a quite extraordinary operational career during the Second World War to add to his previous endeavours during which he had been awarded an impressive array of decorations, which included the Military Cross (MC) and Air Force Cross (AFC) to add to the DFC he had been awarded in Waziristan during the 1920s.

Without seeking permission from his own superiors, Wray continued to fly on operations and to infuse confidence in the young Poles under his command. He was determined to look after them and nurture them through their early period of operations. Despite the fact he needed a walking stick because of his own physical disability and lameness, the result of a wound suffered during the previous war, it did nothing to deter his bravery. Wray is known to have flown on at least thirteen operations while serving as the station commander at Hemswell, even though his chances of escaping a damaged aircraft were next to none. During his first month alone, he flew at least six times with new crews from each of the squadrons. Then, during a raid against Essen on the night of 25/26 March

1942, he flew his Wellington down to a low altitude, despite the heavy defences, in order to correctly identify the target so that bombing accuracy for the main force would be improved.

Wray had displayed a fine example of gallantry and strong leadership. The following month came the announcement that he was to be awarded a Bar to the DFC that he had won nearly twenty years earlier. The Poles were also quick to recognize his quite extraordinary contribution to the war and awarded him the Virtuti Militari in recognition of his outstanding courage and leadership while flying with the two Polish squadrons at Hemswell (see also Binbrook and Grimsby for more about Wray).

In May 1942 300 (Mazowiecki) Squadron moved out to nearby Ingham, a satellite airfield of Hemswell, leaving just 301 in residence. But the squadron was not alone at Hemswell for long as two months later another Polish Wellington unit, 305 (Weilkopolski) Squadron, moved in and six months later 300 returned.

For the first quarter of 1943 the three Polish Wellington squadrons operated together as the Hemswell Wing. One example of the struggle faced by the wing on a regular basis was on the night of 19/20 February 1943 when twenty-four of Hemswell's aircraft formed part of a raiding force of over 300 aircraft sent to attack Wilhelmshaven. Although there were relatively few casualties amongst the bomber squadrons, the raid was a failure. Pathfinder marking of the target was inaccurate, causing most of the bombs from the attacking force to fall to the north of the town. In the case of Hemswell's Wellingtons, seven of the twenty-four aircraft did not even reach the target, six having returned home with technical problems and the seventh having ditched in the North Sea after suffering an engine failure.

In April 301 (Pomorski) Squadron disbanded in preparation for receiving the four-engine Halifax and a move elsewhere, with most of its crews moving across to 300, and soon after the two remaining squadrons moved to Ingham so that Hemswell could be prepared for the arrival of two new heavy squadrons equipped with the four-engine Lancaster.

Hemswell was then developed to the standard pattern design for heavy bombers, with three concrete runways, but the first Lancaster unit to arrive was not an operational squadron but was instead 1 Group's LFS, which arrived in January 1944. Training for a new Lancaster crew would typically last a couple of weeks and at its peak, which occurred during mid-late 1944, the LFS was training up to 130 crews every month.

The LFS remained until November 1944 when it was replaced by two of 1 Group's new Lancaster squadrons: 150 and 170 Squadrons. Hemswell was once again an operational airfield with both newly-arrived squadrons soon flying their first operational sorties with their new types; the first ops were against Karlsruhe on the night of 4/5 December 1944, with all aircraft returning safely to Hemswell.

Both 150 and 170 Squadrons remained at Hemswell until the end of the war, with the airfield having become part of 15 Base, headquartered at Scampton, for this final phase. With hostilities over both squadrons were disbanded before the end of 1945.

Because Hemswell had been an established RAF airfield at the beginning of the war, there were no immediate plans for it to close. Instead, there followed a period when fighters operated from Hemswell as part of 1687 Bomber Defence Training Flight (BDTF) to provide bomber crews with training against a fighter threat. There was also a brief period when the airfield was home to two squadrons of Mosquitos, although they had moved out by the end of 1946. Hemswell then returned to being a bomber airfield with Avro Lincolns before it stepped into the jet age with the arrival of Canberras. However, the airfield was considered unsuitable for further development to accommodate the RAF's new V-bombers entering service and so Hemswell's flying days drew to an end as the Lincolns and Canberras moved out.

But Hemswell's days were not over altogether. From the end of 1959 until 1963 it was home to Thor ballistic missiles during the height of the Cold War, after which it was used for recruit training until 1967 when the last RAF personnel moved out. Since then, Hemswell has been used for a number of different reasons, including being used as a refugee camp for Ugandans during the 1970s.

The former airfield can be found by taking the A15 northbound from Lincoln and turning left at Caenby Corner along the A631 towards Gainsborough. After about two miles, on the northern side of the road at Hemswell Cliff, can be found the entrance to the former airfield and what has now become an antiques

The former airfield of Hemswell is now home to the Hemswell Antiques Centre, which has been established in several of the station's former buildings. (Author)

trading centre. The A631 marks the southern boundary of the former airfield and the B1398 the western boundary.

Considering the RAF moved out nearly fifty years ago, much of Hemswell has survived, including hangars, the former parade ground, barrack accommodation and various other buildings from the former technical and domestic sites. The Hemswell Antiques Centre is established in four of the station's former buildings. A memorial stone erected by the 170 Squadron Association at the former main gate is dedicated to all those who did not return while serving with the squadron at Hemswell during 1944–45. There is also a memorial to commemorate all those who served at Hemswell between 1936 and 1967, and especially those who lost their lives during the Second World War. It can be found in the central part of the Antiques Centre, on the edge of the former parade square adjacent to Barton Road.

Summary of Hemswell during the Second World War

Squadron	Date	Aircraft type
144 Squadron	May 1938–16 July 1941	Blenheim / Hampden
61 Squadron	March 1937–16 July 1941	Blenheim / Hampden

300 (Mazowiecki) Squadron	18 July 1941–17 May 1942	Wellington I/IV
	31 January–21 June 1943	Wellington III
301 (Pomorski) Squadron	18 July 1941–7 April 1943	Wellington I/IV
305 (Weilkopolski) Squadron	23 July 1942–21 June 1943	Wellington IV
150 Squadron	22 November 1944–7 November 1945	Lancaster I/III
170 Squadron	29 November 1944–14 November 1945	Lancaster I/III

CHAPTER SEVEN

Ingham

One of several former airfields located to the north of the city of Lincoln is Ingham, sometimes referred to as Cammeringham as it was by the latter that the airfield became known during the late stages of the Second World War.

Like other sites identified on the Lincoln cliff, Ingham was one of many locations surveyed during the late 1930s as a potential airfield. It was, however, initially considered unsuitable for development but the expansion of Bomber Command and the need for a greater number of squadrons and, therefore, more airfields meant the initial decision was overturned.

Two members of 300 (Mazowiecki) Squadron pictured in a Wellington. The Poles operated various marks of Wellington until 1944 from three of Lincolnshire's airfields, including Ingham. (Author's collection via Ken Delve)

Work began in the early 1940s but the airfield was not constructed with hardened runways, and so it was built to a standard three-runway grass airfield design, with the main runway orientated south-west to north-east and the air traffic control tower unusually positioned between the three runways. There was, however, a hardened perimeter track to link some thirty aircraft hard standings with the runways, and four hangars provided

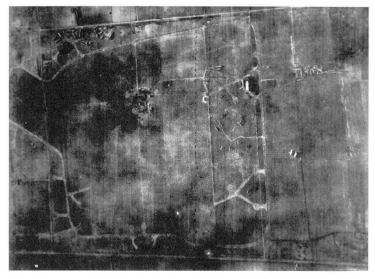

The all-grass airfield of Ingham pictured at the end of the Second World War. The airfield was never suitable for the four-engine heavy bombers and so its use was limited. (Author's collection via Ken Delve)

facilities for the maintenance of the aircraft. Although a number of domestic buildings were built on the airfield, personnel would also be required to make use of a number of buildings in the village of Ingham for domestic and administrative purposes.

Although seemingly ready several months before, it was not until May 1942 that Ingham was officially opened as a satellite airfield for nearby Hemswell as part of 1 Group. The first aircraft to operate from Ingham were the Wellingtons of 300 (Mazowiecki) Squadron. The Poles remained until the early weeks of 1943 when they moved to the main airfield at Hemswell to be replaced by Wellingtons of 199 Squadron. But the new arrivals only stayed for four months before moving out again to make way for the return of 300 (Mazowiecki) Squadron and a second Polish unit, 305 (Weilkopolski) Squadron, which also arrived from Hemswell as work began there in preparation for the arrival of heavy bombers. But 305's stay was only short-lived as less than three months later it moved out.

Like all of Bomber Command's squadrons involved with the hard battles being fought during 1943, the Poles were heavily involved in the main raids. On the night of 8/9 October, 300's Wellingtons were part of an attacking force of more than 500 bombers against Hannover. Conditions were good and so the Pathfinders were able to accurately mark the target, and the raid that followed was the heaviest against the city of the war; all twenty-six of Ingham's Wellingtons returned safely. It was also the last time the Wellingtons were involved with Bomber Command's Main Force and from now on they would only be used for minor operations.

With Ingham being unsuitable for the operation of four-engine heavy bombers, its future as a bomber airfield was limited. The problems of operating from a grass airfield were obvious and facilities on the site were only ever basic to say the least, and with 300 (Mazowiecki) Squadron due to convert to the Lancaster, the squadron moved out in March 1944.

For the rest of the year the airfield was used for non-operational flying and became home to bomber defence training units; specifically 1687 BDTF and 1481 (Bomber) Gunnery Flight, equipped mainly with Miles Martinets and Hawker Hurricanes, with the task of providing target-towing and fighter affiliation training for the bomber crews.

The B1398 Middle Street marks the western part of the former airfield of Ingham and is where some of the old buildings remain. The RAF Ingham Heritage Group plans to ensure the history of this former wartime airfield lives on. (Author)

To avoid confusion with villages of the same name in Norfolk and Suffolk, the official change of name from RAF Ingham to RAF Cammeringham was promulgated in November 1944, although it was a change that would have little effect as the airfield closed to flying in early 1945 and was placed on care and maintenance. With the war over, the airfield was briefly used for technical training and then for accommodating Polish aircrew waiting to be discharged from active duty. The site then reverted to agricultural use once more, although a number of the airfield's wartime buildings remained for several years. Today there are very few reminders of this once active airfield.

The site of the former airfield can be found about seven miles to the north of Lincoln, on the western side of the A15 when heading northbound. After passing Scampton airfield, there is a minor road to the left towards the village of Ingham. This road marks the southern boundary of the former airfield while the B1398 Middle Street (which runs northwards) marks the western edge and the main A15 marks the eastern extremity. A few tracks running through the former airfield remain and the RAF Ingham Heritage Group plans to ensure the history of this airfield lives on by developing a building on the former airfield as a heritage centre.

Summary of Ingham during the Second World War

Squadron	Date	Aircraft type
300 (Mazowiecki) Squadron	18 May 1942–30 January 1943	Wellington IV
	22 June 1943–1 March 1944	Wellington X
199 Squadron	3 February–19 June 1943	Wellington III/X
305 (Weilkopolski) Squadron	22 June–4 September 1943	Wellington X

CHAPTER EIGHT

Kelstern

Located eight miles to the east of Market Rasen, and on one of the highest points of the Lincolnshire Wolds, is the site of the former airfield of Kelstern. It was only used during the last eighteen months of the Second World War and only then because of Bomber Command's increasing needs during its expansion programme of 1942/43.

The area had first been used by the Royal Flying Corps during the First World War and so it was surveyed again during early 1942. Although the original landing ground was considered unsuitable for development as an airfield for heavy bombers, a site about a mile to the north was found to meet the needs, although it was clear even then that the airfield was only ever going to be big enough to accommodate one bomber squadron.

Work began almost straight away but preparing a site for heavy bombers was not easy and required lengthy work. In the end it took nearly eighteen months to complete and required closing the minor road running between the villages of Binbrook and South Elkington. The airfield was built to the standard A-pattern design with three hardened runways, the main one running from the north-east corner of the site to the south-west and the others essentially running north-south and south-east to north-west. The technical site, including a T2 hangar, was located in the north-western part of the airfield, as was the air traffic control tower. There were two other hangars around the site and the aircraft dispersals were mainly on the southern and eastern sides of the airfield, all connected to the runways by a looped perimeter track.

Kelstern eventually opened in August 1943 under the command of Group Captain R H Donkin. For the new arrivals it seemed that all the effort had gone into constructing the runways, perimeter track and hard standings, with little thought given to those who were to serve at the airfield. The priority was clearly, and understandably, on preparing the ground to commence bomber operations as soon as possible rather than on the domestic accommodation, and so the draughty Nissen huts did little to boost morale during the winter months!

Assigned to 1 Group Bomber Command, Kelstern formed part of 12 Base, headquartered at Binbrook and under the overall command of Air Commodore Arthur Wray (see Binbrook, Grimsby and Hemswell for more information about Wray). It was Wray who reportedly flew the first Lancaster into the airfield and he would become a regular visitor to the station.

The airfield was soon declared ready to commence operations and so a new Lancaster squadron, 625 Squadron, was formed at Kelstern at the beginning of October 1943, with its nucleus being made up of experienced crews from 100 Squadron at nearby Grimsby. 625 Squadron flew its first operations on the night of 18/19 October when nine of its aircraft joined a main force of 360 Lancasters tasked with attacking Hannover. It was the last of a series of raids against the city and all of Kelstern's aircraft returned safely.

The squadron had become operational just in time to take part in Bomber Command's main offensive against Berlin, a hard and costly campaign lasting four months. All those at Kelstern worked tirelessly throughout the winter of 1943/44 to keep the airfield open; even when it had been covered in the deepest snow.

Compared with other bomber squadrons, 625 was far from one of the largest. Nonetheless, the squadron managed to send nineteen aircraft to Stuttgart on the night of 15/16 March 1944. They made up part of a large force of 863 aircraft, including more than 600 Lancasters, but amongst the thirty-seven bombers lost that night were two from Kelstern. Then, just over a week later, three of Kelstern's Lancasters were amongst seventy-two bombers lost on the night of 24/25 March from a raiding force of more than 800 aircraft carrying out the last major raid of the winter against Berlin.

These were hard losses to take but the squadron continued to provide as many aircraft as it could as Bomber Command's offensive continued. The squadron also took part in the disastrous raid against Nuremberg on the night of 30/31 March when ninety-five bombers failed to return. Amongst the losses was one of 625's Lancasters flown by 22-year-old Squadron Leader Tom Nicholls. It is believed his aircraft was shot down by a night fighter over Bonn.

As part of the softening of enemy defences ahead of the Allied D-Day landings, the squadron also took part in the ill-fated raid on the night of 3/4 May against a German military camp near the French village of Mailly-le-Camp. More than forty aircraft from a raiding force of 346 Lancasters were lost that night including three from Kelstern.

All these losses had marked a bad few months for the squadron and being such a small station, with just a single unit operating from the airfield, losses at Kelstern would have been felt by all. But everyone carried on, just as they did across all of Bomber Command's airfields in the county, and 625 Squadron delivered more than a thousand tons of bombs for three consecutive months between July and August 1944 in support of the Allied breakout from Normandy. It was a marvellous effort for such a small station.

625 Squadron had now expanded to more than thirty aircraft and three flights of aircrew, and this led to its C Flight forming the nucleus of a new Lancaster unit, 170 Squadron, which re-formed at Kelstern in October 1944. But there was never going to be room to operate the two squadrons together and so 170 moved out to Dunholme Lodge within a matter of days.

In November, 625 Squadron was taken over by Wing Commander John Barker, a pilot who had previously only flown single-engine aircraft. After a very brief one-hour conversion on to the Lancaster, Barker took command of the squadron. Although squadron commanders were only required to fly on operations now and then, Barker immediately endeared himself to the squadron by insisting on flying the next operation with a junior crew. John Barker always led by example and commanded the squadron for the rest of the war. He had the rare distinction of leading both a Spitfire squadron and a Lancaster squadron in combat and remained in the post-war RAF to reach the rank of air vice-marshal.

The winter of 1944/45 proved to be yet another hard one but those at Kelstern coped as ever with just about everything the

Lincolnshire weather could throw at them, although a heavy blizzard did deposit so much snow high up on the Wolds that the airfield was out of action for a short period of three days.

The last operational sorties from Kelstern were flown on 3 April 1945 against a German military barracks near Nordhausen. Two Lancasters failed to return from the raid, including one from 625 Squadron flown by 22-year-old Flight Sergeant Tom Collier; he and his crew were Kelstern's final casualties of the war. The squadron began moving out the following day for its new home at Scampton from where it flew its last operation of the war against the SS barracks at Berchtesgaden on 25 April 1945.

The departure of 625 Squadron brought an end to the brief history of Kelstern airfield. Nearly seventy aircraft had been lost during its operational existence of just eighteen months, a period in which the squadron had taken part in nearly 200 of Bomber Command's raids. For those who served at Kelstern, particularly during the winter months, their lasting memories may well be having to endure the cold and windy conditions high up in the Wolds. But the squadron had done well as its overall loss rate of less than 2 per cent shows; a low casualty rate when compared with other Bomber Command squadrons.

With the war over, the airfield was first placed on care and maintenance and then, in 1946, the site was passed over to the

The memorial to 625 Squadron is believed to be Lincolnshire's first memorial of its type and provides the only real reminder of the once active Bomber Command airfield of Kelstern. (Author)

Ministry of Agriculture. The land was sold and has long since returned to farming, although a number of wartime buildings could still be found for many years. But now, apart from a few lumps of concrete here and there, little, if anything, of the former airfield remains.

The site of the former airfield can be reached by taking the A631 from Market Rasen towards Louth. Between the villages of Ludford and Elkington, take a left turn to Kelstern village. Having passed through the small village, continue to the crossroads of an unclassified road. Binbrook is to the left but take the turning right (to the east) along the small narrow road towards North Elkington. This road takes you through the centre of the former airfield and a memorial stone is immediately on your left. It was erected by the 625 Squadron Association and dedicated in 1964 as a tribute to the men who served with the squadron. This, it is believed, was Lincolnshire's first memorial of its type and provides a reminder of what was once an active Bomber Command airfield.

Summary of Kelstern during the Second World War

Squadron	Date	Aircraft type
625 Squadron	1 October 1943–4 April 1945	Lancaster I/III
170 Squadron	15–21 October 1944	Lancaster I/III

Chapter Nine

Kirmington

About twelve miles to the west of Grimsby is Humberside Airport, once the wartime airfield of Kirmington and home to 166 Squadron.

Built on a large area of flat land, work began in late 1941 and was completed the following summer to the standard Class A design, with three concrete runways; the main one running from north-east to south-west, with the two shorter runways aligned south-west to north-east and east-west. A perimeter track connected the thirty-six hard standings and three main hangars were constructed, two on the western side of the airfield and one on the east, while the domestic and administrative sites were located to the south and around the east side of the village of Kirmington. Because the northern end of the airfield spread across the main A18, the road had to be diverted to run more northwards towards the village of Croxton.

With work complete, Kirmington was first used by training units during 1942 but the airfield officially opened in October 1942 as a satellite of Elsham Wolds and part of 1 Group. The first bomber aircraft to arrive were Wellingtons, which arrived towards the end of the year; the first were those of 150 Squadron, although this squadron was replaced six weeks later by 142 Squadron.

Although 142 moved out soon after, part of the squadron remained to form the nucleus of 166 Squadron, and it was this squadron that was to remain at Kirmington until the end of the war, although the Wellingtons were exchanged for Lancasters during the late summer of 1943.

In its last weeks of operating the Wellington, the squadron was involved in the main bombing campaign against Hamburg, with four raids against the city in ten hectic nights during the end of July and the first few days of August.

The last of these raids was flown on the night of 2/3 August as part of a large mixed force of 740 bombers. Being the summer the Wellingtons did not take off from Kirmington until an hour or so before midnight and being full of fuel, and with a heavy bomb load, the crews were vulnerable to anti-aircraft fire and night fighters at their transit height of 15,000 feet, way below the four-engine heavy bombers. The weather encountered on the way to the target was particularly bad, not at all like the lovely Bank Holiday evening the crews had left behind. They soon encountered large thunderstorms over Germany. They were now in the worst of the weather, with ice beginning to form, and being unable to climb out of the appalling conditions, many turned for home or were recalled. But not all of Kirmington's Wellingtons received the recall message. Some pressed on into the bad weather while others chose to bomb alternative targets instead. The raid was a failure with thirty bombers lost, at least four of which were lost in the bad weather, and only scattered bombing was achieved against the main city.

Lancasters began to arrive at Kirmington during September 1943 and later that month 166 Squadron flew its first operations with its new type. The winter months saw the squadron extensively involved in the hard and costly Battle of Berlin, with the squadron taking part in the sixteen major raids against the Big City, during which nineteen of its aircraft failed to return to Kirmington with the loss of more than a hundred lives; the heaviest losses suffered by a 1 Group squadron of the campaign.

There were further losses, too, when four of the squadron's aircraft were amongst the ninety-five bombers that failed to return from Bomber Command's disastrous raid on Nuremberg on the night of 30/31 March. It had been a bad end to the month. In the space of just a week, nearly half of the squadron had been lost.

There was to be little respite for the squadron during the following months as Bomber Command changed its emphasis from bombing German cities to other targets, in particular enemy lines of communications in northern France in support of the Allied landings in Normandy, and then against the enemy V-weapon sites that had been creating terror and devastation across London and southern England.

During its time at Kirmington, 166 Squadron had on its books at one time or another four centurion Lancasters. One of these, ME746 'AS-R2', known as 'Roger-Squared', remained with the squadron throughout its time on operations, flying continuously from its first op against Cologne on the night of 20/21 April 1944 until the end of the war, by which time it had completed a remarkable 124 ops. The three other centurions were: ED905, which flew nineteen of its eventual 100 ops with the squadron between September 1943 and May 1944; LM550, which flew the first fifty-six of its total 118 ops from Kirmington (May to October 1944); and ME812, which flew the first fifty-three of its 105 ops with the squadron between June and October 1944. ME812 was then

In the passenger terminal at Humberside Airport is the original station bell from Kirmington with a commemorative plaque presented to the airport by the 166 Squadron Association. (Author)

transferred to 153 Squadron, which re-formed at Kirmington after earlier serving in North Africa, although the squadron left for Scampton just a few days later where it would remain for the rest of the war.

166 Squadron remained Kirmington's only resident unit until the end of the war. The squadron's final bombing sorties were flown on 25 April 1945 against Hitler's so-called 'Eagles Nest' and the local SS barracks at Berchtesgaden, after which the squadron took part in Operations *Manna* and *Exodus*, the dropping of food supplies over Holland and the repatriation of Allied prisoners of war.

While operating from Kirmington the squadron had lost more than 150 aircraft, around three-quarters being Lancasters. With

In the village of Kirmington is a memorial garden dedicated to all the men and women who served with 166 Squadron at Kirmington during 1943–45. (Author)

hostilities over the squadron disbanded and Kirmington was placed on care and maintenance. For several years the airfield was maintained until the land finally reverted to agricultural use during the 1950s. However, part of the former airfield was maintained for light aircraft flying and then, during the 1960s, the land and location were considered ideal for development as an airport. The airport finally opened in 1974 and, with a change in county boundaries, it was called Humberside Airport.

The airport can be reached by taking the last junction of the M180 eastbound. Follow the signs eastwards along the A18 and the airport is located to the south of the road just before Kirmington village. In the passenger terminal is the original station bell with a commemorative plaque, which was presented to the airport by the 166 Squadron Association in 1990. In the village church (St Helen) at Kirmington is a memorial plaque and a roll of honour dedicated to the men of 166 Squadron. Also found in the village is a garden and a memorial plaque with the badge of 166 Squadron. It is dedicated to all the men and women who served with the squadron at Kirmington during the period 1943–45, of whom 921 gave their lives.

Summary of Kirmington during the Second World War

Squadron	Date	Aircraft type
150 Squadron	October–18 December 1942	Wellington III
142 Squadron	19 December 1942–27 January 1943	Wellington III
166 Squadron	27 January 1943–18 November 1945	Wellington III / Lancaster I/III
153 Squadron	7–14 October 1944	Lancaster I/III

CHAPTER TEN

Ludford Magna

Five miles to the east of Market Rasen is the village of Ludford. Just to the south of the village is the former airfield of Ludford Magna, home to the Lancasters of 101 Squadron, a rather specialist unit and the airfield's only residents during the Second World War.

The 1 Group airfield of Ludford Magna was opened in June 1943 under the command of Group Captain Bobby Blucke, a veteran of the First World War. As a pilot he had become involved in the early trials and development of radar, working at the Royal Aircraft Establishment during the mid-1930s. Then, when the Second World War broke out, he had commanded the Blind Approach Training and Development Unit and then the Wireless Investigation Development Unit before commanding a bomber station in Yorkshire.

With this background, Blucke was the ideal man to take command of the new station of Ludford Magna, for the airfield was to have a specialist role during the bombing campaigns ahead. Lancasters of 101 Squadron moved in almost immediately and were soon in action over Germany. It was the height of Bomber Command's offensive against industrial targets in the Ruhr.

There were other targets as well and during one raid against Hannover on the night of 27/28 September 1943, two members of the same crew were awarded the Conspicuous Gallantry Medal (CGM) for their bravery. Awarded only to non-commissioned officers, the CGM was a comparable award to the DSO awarded to officers and was first awarded in 1943. Considering only 103 awards were made during the Second World War, to have two members of the same crew decorated with the CGM is rare.

A Lancaster of 101 Squadron being bombed up ahead of another night raid. (AHB)

The two men were the pilot, Arthur Walker, and his flight engineer, Stan Meyer. While running in to their aiming point at Hannover, their Lancaster had become coned by searchlights and then attacked by a night fighter. In the attack that followed, their aircraft was badly damaged and an engine set on fire. As Walker threw the bomber into a dive a fire broke out in the fuselage. Meyer immediately set about trying to extinguish the fire until he was overcome by fumes. Having been dragged clear, Meyer then provided Walker with support while they went on to bomb the target before taking the crippled bomber home. It was bravery typical of so many bomber crews, not just at Ludford Magna but all across Bomber Command.

It was around this time that 101 Squadron was selected for the specialist role of radio countermeasures. To help cause confusion and to counter the German night fighter threat, the squadron's aircraft were equipped with the highly secret Airborne Cigar equipment, simply known as ABC. This specialist equipment was designed to jam the communications frequencies used by the German night fighters and included three transmitters and a receiver. The three transmitters fitted to the modified Lancasters were simply three aerials. They were quite distinctive and easily identified; two were on top of the fuselage with the third under the nose.

The equipment was fitted from October, although not all of the squadron's aircraft were ABC-equipped. Even those that had been were still required to carry a bomb load, typically around 1,000 lb less than the main force bombers to take into account the weight of the specialist equipment and its special duties operator, a fluent German speaker who sat at a table fitted in the fuselage just above the bomb bay with the task of listening to the German night fighter radio frequencies.

These specially equipped Lancasters were first used on the night of 7/8 October 1943 during a raid against Stuttgart. In the early days of ABC the operator transmitted false information in German to the night fighter pilots. However, the Germans soon became aware of this 'spoof' tactic and countered it by broadcasting information across several different frequencies. Therefore, the later tactic employed by the special duties operator was to jam the frequencies in use to prevent the night fighter crews from receiving any transmitted information informing them of where the bombers were.

At that stage of the war, the aircraft and crews of 101 Squadron were all that Bomber Command had to fulfil this role, although it would not be long before a specialist group, 100 Group, would be formed to undertake the increasingly complex world of electronic warfare and countermeasures within one organization. The role of these specially equipped aircraft was considered so vital that the squadron's ABC Lancasters took part in every major Bomber Command raid until the end of the war, even when 1 Group's other squadrons were not involved.

It is not surprising that the squadron's specialist aircraft soon became prime targets for the German night fighters as they were able to home-in on the jamming frequency being used and this often led to high losses for the squadron. Indeed, the squadron had not got off to a good start in its specialist role after the first two aircraft to be equipped with ABC were both lost on operations.

In addition to the losses, Ludford Magna was a desolate and hastily prepared airfield, and seemed, to some at least, to be one of the worst postings within 1 Group. Being high up on the Lincolnshire Wolds, the airfield was often subject to the worst of weather conditions and its location made it prone to becoming very muddy and boggy during periods of heavy rain. Furthermore, because of its location and varying winds high up in the Wolds, Ludford's main runway had been aligned north–south and this invariably led to problems for the Lancaster crews when having to land in high cross winds.

The combination of the harsh weather and 101 Squadron's vital role meant that Ludford Magna was selected to be the first of a number of Lincolnshire's airfields to be installed with FIDO (see the Introduction for a description of FIDO). Ludford Magna had now become the headquarters of 14 Base under Bomber Command's reorganization, with Ludford given administrative control of its two satellites at Faldingworth and Wickenby.

The hard winter of 1943/44 also marked the height of the Battle of Berlin, a campaign that cost Ludford more than twenty aircraft and crews, but the worst night was still to come. As with many other Bomber Command squadrons, the raid against Nuremberg on the night of 30/31 March 1944 was a disastrous night. 101 Squadron had provided twenty-six ABC-equipped

Not all landings were perfect! An ABC-equipped Lancaster (note ABC aerials) of 101 Squadron pictured on returning from a raid against Augsburg on the night of 25/26 February 1944. (101 Sqn records)

Lancasters to support the raid but seven failed to return. The first enemy night fighters had appeared even before the main force had crossed the Belgian border and for the next hour several combats raged; eighty-two of the ninety-five bombers were lost on the way to the target.

In a single night nearly one-third of 101 Squadron had been lost but the difficult times were far from over as Bomber Command transferred its attention to supporting the build-up to the forthcoming Allied landings. This involved bombing various targets in northern France to destroy and disrupt the enemy's lines of communications and to attack soft targets such as concentrations of enemy forces. One such raid was against the German military camp near the French village of Mailly-le-Camp on the night of 3/4 May 1944 but forty-two of the 346 Lancasters taking part in the raid were lost (12 per cent), including five from Ludford.

During the early hours of D-Day the Lancasters of 101 Squadron were airborne overhead the Channel to disrupt any attempt by the enemy's night fighters to hassle the transport aircraft carrying paratroopers to the invasion area. One of the squadron's aircraft taking part in these operations was DV245 'SR-S Sugar', known affectionately at Ludford as 'The Saint'. Since flying its first op in October 1943, this legendary

In the centre of the village of Ludford, on the main A631, is a granite memorial stone dedicated to the men of 101 Squadron. (Author)

Lanc would go on to complete 122 ops, all with 101 Squadron at Ludford. It had survived nine raids against Berlin and the disastrous Nuremberg raid, but would fall just weeks before the end of the war when it failed to return from a raid against Bremen on 23 March 1945.

Ludford also boasted a second centurion. This was DV302 'SR-H Harry', which flew alongside 'The Saint' from the time 'Harry' carried out its first op in November 1943. 'Harry' was just two ops behind 'The Saint' when the latter completed its own century of missions but 'Harry' passed the impressive milestone in January 1945 and went on to complete 121 ops by the end of the war.

With the war over, 101 Squadron moved out to nearby Binbrook and Ludford Magna was placed on care and maintenance. As with some of the other Bomber Command airfields in Lincolnshire, Ludford Magna was used in the late 1950s and early 1960s as a Thor missile site, after which the airfield closed and the land reverted to agriculture.

The site of the former airfield can be reached by taking the A631 from Market Rasen towards Louth. Just before the village of Ludford, take a right turn along the B1225 and after about a mile the road passes along the western boundary of the former airfield. In the centre of the village of Ludford, on the A631, is a granite memorial stone dedicated in 1978 to the men of 101 Squadron. It was appropriately unveiled by Air Vice-Marshal Bobby Blucke, Ludford Magna's first station commander. Close to the memorial on the main road is the village church (St Mary and St Peter), where the 101 Squadron and 101 Squadron Association standards are kept, as is the Roll of Honour to the squadron.

Summary of Ludford Magna during the Second World War

Squadron	Date	Aircraft type
101 Squadron	15 June 1943–30 September 1945	Lancaster I/III

CHAPTER ELEVEN

North Killingholme

Twelve miles to the north-west of Grimsby is the site of the former airfield of North Killingholme, another of Bomber Command's airfields to only see operational service during the latter period of the war. The airfield was only ever home to one resident bomber squadron and was the last of the new airfields to have been developed during the command's expansion programme of 1943.

The site, however, was originally used by the Royal Naval Air Service during the First World War. But having closed in 1919 the airfield's flying days were seemingly over until the land was surveyed and considered suitable for development as another bomber airfield during the Second World War.

North Killingholme finally opened in November 1943 and allocated to 1 Group. Just weeks later the first Lancasters of 550 Squadron moved in from Grimsby, having formed from C Flight of 100 Squadron, under the command of Wing Commander Jimmy Bennett. 550 Squadron had already flown some operations while at Grimsby and so many of those transferred to North Killingholme were already some way into their operational tour. But the stark contrast from the relative comforts of Grimsby, with the town nearby, to the new airfield at North Killingholme, with its basic facilities and remoteness, came as a bit of a shock, not helped by the fact that their transfer had taken place during the height of what was a bitterly cold winter!

Being the newest of 1 Group's airfields, North Killingholme had been built with concrete runways and hardened dispersals, but any rainfall caused the rest of the airfield to become, in places, a sea of mud. Taxying or manoeuvring a heavy Lancaster around the airfield in the dark was not easy and there was

North Killingholme pictured at the end of the war. (Author's collection via Ken Delve)

always the risk of a wheel slipping off the edge of the hardened surface to bog the aircraft down.

North Killingholme was certainly remote. There was nothing between the airfield and the bank of the Humber estuary in this wind-swept corner of North Lincolnshire. But despite the remoteness and basic conditions, Jimmy Bennett proved to be a popular leader. He was now on his third operational tour with Bomber Command and always believed in enduring the same harsh conditions as those under his command. Under his leadership the squadron would expand over the coming months from a single flight with just a handful of aircraft and crews to a fully equipped squadron of more than thirty Lancasters.

550's introduction to operations from their new home occurred during the height of the Battle of Berlin in the hard winter nights of early 1944. The squadron visited the Big City several times during its early weeks and then, at the end of March 1944, the squadron sent seventeen Lancasters on the disastrous Nuremberg raid. Few squadrons survived unscathed that night and 550 was no different. Amongst the ninety-five bombers that failed to return home were two Lancasters from North Killingholme.

It had been a difficult introduction to ops with fifty of the squadron's aircrew killed but this figure was comparably low compared with other squadrons and reflects the experience level amongst 550's crews. Besides, the squadron was now dropping a greater tonnage of bombs than any other 1 Group squadron at that time.

Jimmy Bennett handed over command of the squadron to 30-year-old Wing Commander Patrick Connolly in May 1944. Final preparations for the Allied landings of north-west Europe were now under way and during the night of 5/6 June the squadron took part in operations to soften up the enemy's coastal defences along the northern coastline of France as a prelude to the Allied landings in Europe. The bombs dropped just before midnight by one of the squadron's Lancasters, LL811 'BQ-J Jig', flown by one of the squadron's original members, 21-year-old Flying Officer Kenyon Bowen-Bravery, are acknowledged to be the first bombs dropped by Bomber Command during Operation *Overlord* to mark the beginning of D-Day.

Even after the Allies had gone safely ashore and started breaking out of the Normandy beachhead towards Germany, the war was far from won and there were, sadly, to be many casualties before victory was in sight. These included the squadron commander, Pat Connolly, who was killed in July, and his replacement, 27-year-old Alan Sisley, who was killed at the end of August during a daylight attack against a V2 rocket site.

Although 550 Squadron and North Killingholme both had relatively short operational lives, the airfield was home to three legendary Lancs at one time or another. The squadron's most famous Lancaster was EE139, which had been transferred from 100 Squadron to 550 while it was in the process of forming at Grimsby at the end of 1943. Known as the 'Phantom of the Ruhr', the Lancaster bore the nose art of a grim-looking hooded skeleton figure reaching over clouds to drop bombs. Even the bomb tally was recorded in rows of thirteen with raids against Italian targets being recorded as ice cream cones instead of bombs to represent each raid. But it didn't do the 'Phantom's' luck any harm. EE139 survived the war having flown a total of

121 ops, before the aircraft was eventually struck off charge in February 1946.

550 had two other centurions on its books during 1944. One was ED905 'F-Fox', which arrived at North Killingholme in June 1944 having already flown nearly fifty operational sorties; 'F-Fox' flew its 100th op in November before it was retired from operational service and sent to a training unit. The other Lancaster to have completed the milestone 100 ops was PA995, which had also been delivered to North Killingholme in June. PA995 was a new aircraft, though, and so was given the letter 'K' but was then re-designated as 'V-Victor'. A large vulture was painted on its nose with 'The Vulture Strikes!' written just above. The aircraft flew all 100 of its ops with the squadron from North Killingholme, although its luck ran out on its next, and 101st, operational sortie; it failed to return from a raid against Dessau on the night of 7/8 March 1945 with the loss of three of its crew.

With bombing raids over, the squadron then flew on Operation *Manna*, the dropping of food supplies over Holland, and Operation *Exodus*, the repatriation of prisoners of war, before 550 Squadron disbanded in October 1945, less than two years after it had been formed. During its sixteen months of

The former airfield of North Killingholme lies to the west of the village where there is now an industrial estate. At the entrance to the estate (appropriately named Lancaster Approach) is a memorial to 550 Squadron, which is now part of the Northern Lincolnshire Aviation Heritage Trail. (Author)

operational life at North Killingholme the squadron had flown more than 3,500 sorties on nearly 200 of Bomber Command's major raids, during which more than 16,000 tons of bombs had been dropped. But it had cost the squadron nearly sixty aircraft and many crews, although the squadron's overall loss rate of less than 2 per cent was amongst the lowest in Bomber Command. North Killingholme then closed to flying and the land was sold for industrial development, although several of the wartime buildings remained for many years.

The site of the former airfield can be reached by taking the M180 and then the A180 towards Grimsby. About three miles before Immingham take the A160 towards the industrial area of Immingham and South Killingholme. At the village of South Killingholme take the turning left to North Killingholme and the former airfield lies to the west of the village and is now an industrial estate. A road onto the estate is appropriately named Lancaster Approach as this marks an access road to the former airfield. On the corner of Lancaster Approach is a memorial stone with the badge of 550 Squadron and a translation of the squadron's motto 'Through Fire We Conquer'. In the village church (St Denys) is a squadron badge and a plaque dedicated to the men of 550 Squadron. The plaque was given to the village by Wing Commander Jimmy Bennett DFC and Bar, the squadron's first commanding officer, as a token of esteem and reciprocation for the kindness and co-operation shown by the village to the squadron during its time at North Killingholme between 1944 and 1945.

Summary of North Killingholme during the Second World War

Squadron	Date	Aircraft type
550 Squadron	3 January 1944–31 October 1945	Lancaster I/III

CHAPTER TWELVE

Sandtoft

The airfield of Sandtoft lies just inside the north-western boundary of northern Lincolnshire. The land was first surveyed by the Air Ministry during early 1942 and found potentially suitable for the new four-engine heavy bombers entering service with Bomber Command. Work started later in the year with the original intention of developing Sandtoft as an operational airfield of 1 Group with the target date of early 1944 being set for the commencement of operations.

Like all main bomber airfields, it would take several months for construction work to be complete and so, in the meantime, Sandtoft prepared for the arrival of a HCU. Until that phase of the war, the training of bomber crews was carried out at

Sandtoft Flying Club now occupies part of the former wartime airfield, then home to 1667 Heavy Conversion Unit, where many Bomber Command crews were trained during the latter period of the war. (Author)

squadron level but the greater demand for more crews as Bomber Command expanded resulted in the establishment of specialist training units made up of experienced instructors drawn from the squadrons.

With each of Bomber Command's groups assuming responsibility for the training of its own crews, 1 Group's training task fell to RAF Lindholme in South Yorkshire with airfields just across the county border in northern Lincolnshire, such as Sandtoft, being allocated new training units to relieve the training burden on Lindholme.

Although Sandtoft was still not complete, the airfield opened in December 1943 as a satellite of 11 Base at Lindholme. The first aircraft to arrive were Halifaxes of 1667 HCU, which moved in during February 1944. These formed the first flight but soon after two more flights were formed, and by the end of the year there was even a fourth flight formed to train the instructors at Sandtoft as well as those at the other HCUs at Lindholme and Blyton.

Although the Halifax proved a suitable training platform for the crews of Bomber Command, the truth was that many of the airframes at Sandtoft were tired and underpowered. They had been released by the operational squadrons in favour of the Lancasters and by the end of the war, even the HCU's Halifaxes had been replaced by Lancasters.

As with the other 1 Group training airfields in northern Lincolnshire, Sandtoft was transferred to 7 (Training) Group during the latter months of the war. The new training group had responsibility for the training of all Bomber Command crews but by early 1945 there were more than enough to fill the front-line squadrons, and so this led to a drawdown in the training task at Sandtoft as the war approached its final phase.

With the Second World War over, Sandtoft was placed on care and maintenance. In the early 1950s the airfield was briefly handed over to the Americans for possible development as part of the build-up of American forces in Britain during the early years of the Cold War. But no American forces ever occupied the site and the airfield was handed back to the Air Ministry in the mid-1950s for disposal. Part of the former wartime airfield has survived and is now used by the Sandtoft Flying Club for private flying, while other areas are used for industrial purposes, some of which support the Humber ports.

The airfield is adjacent to the southern side of the M180, approximately twelve miles to the north-east of Doncaster, between Scunthorpe and Thorne, and on the eastern side of the village of Sandtoft. Belton Road, which runs eastwards from the village of Sandtoft and then becomes Sandtoft Road, passes straight through the site of the former wartime airfield. The flying club occupies the southern side of the road while the industrial park is to the north. The M180 marks the northern edge of the former airfield while the River Thorne marks its eastern boundary.

CHAPTER THIRTEEN

Sturgate

O ne of the last airfields to be developed during the Second World War was Sturgate, another airfield constructed for 1 Group as part of Bomber Command's expansion plans during the latter years of the Second World War. But, having not been completed until March 1944, and with so many other airfields already in existence across the area, Sturgate effectively became surplus to requirements and was opened too late to see operational service.

With no front-line squadron or HCU allocated to Sturgate, the airfield was first used as a relief landing ground for the

One of the last bomber airfields to be developed during the Second World War, Sturgate was not completed until 1944, by which time it was considered surplus to requirements and was opened too late to see operational service. However, part of the airfield has survived, including the original air traffic control tower, which is now home to the Lincoln Aero Club. (Author)

LFS at Hemswell. Lancasters soon became regular visitors to the airfield before, in September 1944, Sturgate finally received its first resident unit. But the new arrivals were not Lancasters and were, instead, twin-engine Airspeed Oxfords of 1520 BATF. Sturgate was also home to 1 Group's Aircrew Training School, a holding unit for crews waiting for a course at an HCU, which remained at the airfield with the BAT Flight until February 1945.

Sturgate did eventually receive two squadrons of Lancasters, 50 and 61 from Skellingthorpe, but it was not until after the war. The two squadrons only stayed for six months before moving to Waddington in January 1946, after which the airfield at Sturgate closed. The airfield did open again, though, and was used by the Americans as a transit airfield for units of Strategic Air Command during the latter half of the 1950s and early 1960s.

Part of the former wartime airfield of Sturgate has survived and is currently used by Eastern Air Executive and the Lincoln Aero Club. The airfield is about five miles to the south-east of Gainsborough and the entrance can be found off Common Lane between the small villages of Heapham and Upton. The former wartime air traffic control tower is still in use and is now home to the Aero Club.

CHAPTER FOURTEEN

Wickenby

Eleven miles to the north-east of Lincoln is the airfield of Wickenby, another former Bomber Command airfield still in use today and a popular place of interest.

Having been identified in 1941 as a suitable site for development of a bomber airfield, work was carried out in relatively quick time so that Wickenby was ready for opening in the summer of 1942. The road connecting the villages of Holton cum Beckering

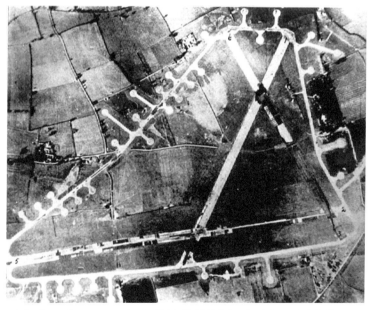

Wickenby under construction in 1942. (RAF Wickenby Memorial Collection via Anne Law)

and Snelland had to be closed in order to construct the airfield, which was designed to the standard Bomber Command layout with three concrete runways and a perimeter track. The main runway ran east–west along the southern side of the airfield with the two other runways, aligned south-west to north-east and south-east to north-west, crossing towards the northern part of the airfield. Thirty-six hard standings were linked by a perimeter track and two T2 hangars were built, one on the northern part of the airfield and the other to the south of the main runway, while the technical and main domestic sites were built on the eastern part of the airfield and extended towards the village of Holton cum Beckering.

Wickenby was initially under the command of Wing Commander Dabinett and allocated to 1 Group as a satellite for Binbrook. The first resident unit was 12 Squadron, which moved its Wellingtons in from Binbrook during September 1942.

Unlike many other squadrons, 12 was to be spared from being moved around and so the squadron was to remain at Wickenby for the rest of the war. But few Wellington sorties were flown from the airfield as 12 Squadron was the second of 1 Group's squadrons to convert to the four-engine Lancaster. The first of

Lancasters and crews of 12 and 626 Squadrons pictured at Wickenby in 1944. (RAF Wickenby Memorial Collection via Anne Law)

An unusual picture but perhaps typical of how station personnel found time to relax during the hectic bombing campaigns. This is the Ad Astra Concert Party, taken at Wickenby in 1944. (RAF Wickenby Memorial Collection via Anne Law)

the new heavy bombers started to arrive in November and by early January 1943 the squadron commenced operations with the type when nine of the squadron's aircraft made up part of a raiding force of more than fifty Lancasters tasked with attacking an oil refinery at the German city of Essen.

Over the next few weeks the squadron continued to expand in size and was able to play a full part in the Battle of the Ruhr, which lasted until the summer of 1943. During one of these raids, against Düsseldorf on the night of 11/12 June, Wickenby suffered its worst night of the war so far when five of the squadron's twenty-four Lancasters taking part in the raid failed to return.

The Battle of Hamburg followed and then the Battle of Berlin. It was the start of the campaign against the Nazi capital that saw the arrival of a second Lancaster squadron at Wickenby. This was 626 Squadron, a new squadron, which formed at Wickenby in November 1943. As with other Bomber Command squadrons formed during the latter period of the war, the history of 626 Squadron is very brief. It was in existence for less than two years and Wickenby was its only home.

To be able to accommodate a second heavy bomber squadron meant that facilities at the airfield had to be expanded, with the airfield's domestic site now covering a large area that extended as far as the villages of Fulnetby and Rand. Wickenby was now a sub-station of 14 Base, headquartered at Ludford Magna.

Between the two squadrons, Wickenby was able to send thirty or more aircraft a night on raids. But with large numbers came large losses and Wickenby's worst night during this period was on the night of 3/4 May 1944, when seven aircraft failed to return from the raid against a German military camp near the French village of Mailly-le-Camp.

The two Wickenby squadrons continued to operate side-by-side in support of the Allied landings in Normandy in June 1944 and then the subsequent advance into north-west Europe. The squadrons' personnel remained very close during their time at Wickenby and even though victory was in sight, the losses continued; the last loss occurred on 12 April 1945, just weeks before the end of the war, when three aircraft failed to return from a raid against an oil refinery at Luzendorf.

Both squadrons then took part in the final raid of the war against Hitler's Eagle's Nest and the SS barracks at Berchtesgaden on 25 April 1945. One Lancaster taking part in

The wartime control tower at Wickenby is still in use today. Not only does it provide control for private flying at the airfield but the tower is also open to visitors to view the excellent Wickenby Memorial Collection. (Author)

A memorial to 12 and 626 Squadrons stands at the entrance to Wickenby airfield. (Author)

this final raid was ME758 'PH-N Nan', an aircraft that had first been delivered to Wickenby in early 1944 and flew its first op against Lyons at the beginning of May. By the time it returned from Berchtesgaden nearly a year later, it had completed its 106th op with 12 Squadron.

With hostilities over the squadrons took part in Operations *Manna* and *Dodge*, the dropping of food supplies over Holland and the repatriation of prisoners of war from Europe. 12 Squadron then returned to Binbrook in September and 626 disbanded the following month. During their time at Wickenby the two squadrons had lost more than 150 Lancasters.

With the Lancasters gone, Wickenby was briefly home to a Mosquito squadron before the airfield closed to flying. It was, however, used as a maintenance unit until the mid-1950s when it finally closed, with most of the land reverting to agriculture, although part of the former airfield was developed in the 1960s for private flying. The northern part of the airfield remains in use for light aircraft flying and, remarkably, the original air traffic control tower is still in use.

The airfield can be reached by taking the A158 from Lincoln towards Horncastle. At Bullington take the B1399 through Fulnetby and about a mile further on a minor road to the left passes through the former airfield. The boundaries of the former wartime airfield are marked by several minor roads and the villages of Wickenby to the north-west, Fulnetby to the south, Snelland to the west and Holton cum Beckering to the east.

The entrance to Wickenby airfield is on the minor road between the villages of Snelland and Holton cum Beckering. At the entrance is a memorial dedicated to 12 and 626 Squadrons. It stands on part of the old perimeter track in memory of 1,080 men of the two squadrons who gave their lives on operations from the airfield in the offensive against Germany and the liberation of occupied Europe. The air traffic control tower is also an excellent Visitors' Centre and home to the RAF Wickenby Memorial Collection. The tower is open daily and can be visited without prior permission.

Summary of Wickenby during the Second World War

Squadron	Date	Aircraft type
12 Squadron	25 September 1942–24 September 1945	Wellington/ Lancaster
626 Squadron	7 November 1943–14 October 1945	Lancaster I/III

PART II

Airfields of 5 Group: Central and South Lincolnshire

CHAPTER FIFTEEN

Bardney

Ten miles to the east of Lincoln is the site of the former airfield of Bardney, the wartime home of 9 Squadron, one of the most prestigious squadrons of Bomber Command. The site was first surveyed by the Air Ministry for potential development as an airfield as early as 1941 when it was recognized that Bomber Command would need a significant increase in its

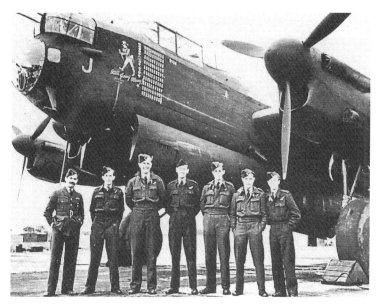

The legendary Lanc 'Johnny Walker' with James Melrose and his crew. Melrose flew the aircraft throughout his tour of operations with 9 Squadron at Bardney, including the aircraft's milestone 100th operational sortie against the mighty German battleship Tirpitz *in September 1944.* (via the Lincolnshire Echo)

number of squadrons and, therefore, more airfields. The land was flat and relatively easy to work and so the decision was made to develop Bardney as a satellite of nearby Waddington, a main airfield of 5 Group Bomber Command.

Construction began in 1942 with the airfield being built to the standard bomber Class A design with three concrete runways, perimeter track, thirty-six pan-type hard standings and three main hangars. The main runway ran almost east–west with the two subsidiary runways aligned south-east to north-west and almost south-west to north-east. Three hangars, two of the T2-type and one B1, were situated around the airfield. The bomb storage site was in the north-east part of the airfield and the domestic site was to the south where, eventually, some 2,500 station personnel were accommodated.

With so much to do it took some time to complete and so Bardney did not open until April 1943. The first aircraft to operate from the new airfield were Lancasters of 9 Squadron, which moved in from Waddington the same month. The squadron had arrived in time for what would later be known as the Battle of the Ruhr, and would remain at the airfield until the end of the war. It was the start of a long association between the squadron and the village of Bardney.

The campaign against industrial targets in the Ruhr was followed by the Battle of Hamburg which, in turn, led to the hardest campaign of them all – the Battle of Berlin, which did not conclude until the end of March 1944. By now Bardney had been given full station status within the 53 Base structure and was under the command of Group Captain Tony Evans-Evans.

It had been a hard first year for 9 Squadron at Bardney. Losses had been high and amongst those killed during a raid against Frankfurt on the night of 22/23 March 1944 was Flying Officer Albert Manning. His aircraft was one of twenty-six Lancasters that failed to return. Flying with Manning that night, and also killed in the raid, was Bardney's new station commander, Group Captain Norman Pleasance, who had just taken over from Evans-Evans.

Despite the losses, one Lancaster to come through this period relatively unscathed was the legendary 'Johnny Walker'. Built by the Metropolitan Vickers plant at Trafford Park, this Lancaster Mark I, with the serial number W4964, was delivered to 9 Squadron at Bardney in April 1943 when the squadron made its move from Waddington.

Given the squadron code 'WS-J Johnny', the aircraft's nose-art was the symbol of the Johnny Walker whisky firm with its motto 'Still Going Strong' beneath it. 'Johnny Walker' flew its first operational sortie to Stettin on the night of 20/21 April. Flown that night by Warrant Officer W E Wood as part of a raiding force of 339 bombers, the aircraft and crew returned safely. One of the aircraft's regular crews during its early months was that of Pilot Officer Charles Newton, a sergeant at the start of his tour, who flew the aircraft fifteen times between July 1943 and January 1944 during the height of the Battles of Hamburg and Berlin. It then became the regular mount of Pilot Officer P E Plowright, a sergeant pilot when he first commenced his tour of operations. Plowright flew the aircraft eighteen times until May 1944, the last twelve of which were flown consecutively to complete his crew's successful tour of operations and earning Plowright the DFC.

'Johnny Walker' was then transferred to a new crew on the night of 19/20 May. The target was Tours in central France and Plowright took with him that night one of the squadron's new pilots, Pilot Officer James Melrose, so that Melrose could gain operational experience as the second pilot, a position known to the crews as the 'second Dickie'. At that stage of the war Bomber Command was helping soften up enemy defences in northern France ahead of the D-Day landings and to attack the enemy's lines of communications to prevent German reinforcements from reaching the beachhead once the landings had taken place. On that particular night Bomber Command sent raiding forces to attack a number of targets, eight in all, and so the aircraft and crews of 9 Squadron were part of a relatively small force of Lancasters tasked with attacking the railway installations in the centre of Tours. It was a follow-on raid from an earlier attack against railway yards on the outskirts of the city and this latter raid proved a success, with much damage caused to the railways and with no aircraft lost.

Melrose and his crew then took 'Johnny Walker' on twenty-two more ops, including the aircraft's 100th operational sortie against the mighty German battleship *Tirpitz* in September 1944. The *Tirpitz* had always been a major concern to the

British and the Admiralty now believed she was about to leave the Kåfjord in northern Norway and put to sea. If *Tirpitz* was allowed to sail then she posed a significant threat to the Royal Navy's Arctic convoys that were providing vital supplies to the Soviet Union.

To attack such a large ship required a specialist weapon, the 12,000 lb Tallboy (see Bomber Command in Second World War for more about Tallboy). It was just what was needed but when armed with a Tallboy the Lancaster did not have the range to reach the fjord from a British base, and so the Russians provided an airfield at Yagodnik near Archangel, still some 600 miles from *Tirpitz* but it was an airfield from where the raid could be carried out.

The raid on *Tirpitz*, called Operation *Paravane*, was to be carried out by a combined force of Lancasters; eighteen from 9 Squadron, led by Wing Commander James Bazin, and twenty aircraft from 617 Squadron based at nearby Woodhall Spa led by Wing Commander Willie Tait (see Woodhall Spa for further details of the raid). Included in 9 Squadron's crews was James Melrose, now a flight lieutenant, and his crew, flying 'Johnny Walker'.

After first flying from Bardney to Lossiemouth, the thirty-eight Lancasters set off for Russia. One was forced to return but the remainder pressed on across the North Sea. They eventually arrived at Yagodnik after a flight of more than ten hours, although a dozen had arrived to find the airfield obscured by cloud and rain and had to divert elsewhere; six were left with no option but to come down in marshland.

In addition to the Lancasters, two B-24 Liberators had taken the squadron's ground crew to Russia and a Mosquito had also made the journey to carry out a reconnaissance mission ahead of the raid and then the post-raid assessment after the raid had been carried out.

By 14 September, those aircraft that had not made it to Yagodnik, and had been fortunate to find an airfield to land rather than come down in the marshes, were recovered to join the rest of the squadron. Some had sustained damage but enough were now ready to take part in the raid.

The weather was favourable for the following day and after the Mosquito returned from its early morning reconnaissance sortie to confirm *Tirpitz* was still there, and that the weather was suitable, the decision was made to carry out the attack. But with the mighty battleship anchored in a narrow fjord, surrounded by a complex and highly effective smoke screen arrangement that could hide the ship in just a matter of minutes, as well as being protected by a number of anti-aircraft guns in addition to those on board *Tirpitz*, the mighty battleship would be a difficult target to hit.

Twenty-eight aircraft were fit to take part in the raid. Twenty of them were carrying Tallboys and seven carried 500 lb Johnny Walker mines, a weapon specifically designed for attacking ships in shallow water. The one other aircraft was to be used to film the raid.

The Lancasters got airborne and their arrival overhead the fjord caught everyone by surprise. There were no fighters to be seen and the flak was largely ineffective but *Tirpitz* soon became obscured by the smoke screen. Seventeen Tallboys were dropped, as were all the Johnny Walker mines, and all aircraft returned safely to Yagodnik.

Just two hours later the Mosquito flew overhead the fjord to carry out the post-raid reconnaissance but a build-up of cloud obscured the area and so it was impossible to assess the raid. All that could be determined was that *Tirpitz* was still afloat, although it was later evident that there had been some damage to the ship; enough to prevent the mighty battleship from putting to sea.

The Lancasters returned to the UK, although one of 617's aircraft was lost over Norway on its way home. As for the legendary 'Johnny Walker', it had survived its trip to Russia and the raid on *Tirpitz*, but was rested from bombing operations the following month having completed 106 ops.

Despite its apparent lack of seaworthiness, *Tirpitz* remained a high priority. It was later discovered that she had been moved south to a fjord near Tromsø for use as a heavy artillery battery. This move south meant the mighty battleship could now be reached from Lossiemouth in northern Scotland and so a second attack on *Tirpitz*, Operation *Obviate*, took place on 29 October. Thirty-seven Lancasters, eighteen from each of 9 and 617 Squadrons plus the aircraft carrying the film unit, took part in the raid, but heavy cloud that had built up shortly before the bombers arrived obscured the target. Although thirty-two aircraft bombed, no Tallboys hit the battleship.

Finally, a third attack against the *Tirpitz*, Operation *Catechism*, took place on 12 November 1944. This time a mixed 9 and 617 force of thirty Lancasters plus the film unit took part. The weather was clear and *Tirpitz* was hit by at least two Tallboys, causing the mighty battleship to capsize once and for all. Several messages of congratulations arrived at both squadrons from the highest levels, including the King, who said 'please convey my hearty congratulations to all those who took part in the daring and successful attack on the *Tirpitz*', and from the Prime Minister, Winston Churchill, who offered his 'heartiest congratulations to all'.

While 9 Squadron had been occupied with the raids against *Tirpitz*, there was a short period during October and November 1944 when two other units were briefly based at Bardney. Firstly, 227 Squadron re-formed at Bardney with Lancasters and personnel from one flight of 9 Squadron, but the new squadron moved out just two weeks later. Then, 189 Squadron re-formed at Bardney, again using Lancasters and more personnel from 9 Squadron, only to move out during early November.

With the two other squadrons having formed and then moved out, it was left to 9 Squadron to continue the battle against Nazi Germany from Bardney. The squadron had now become something of a specialist bombing unit within Bomber Command, using its Tallboys whenever and wherever the need arose.

There were many heroic acts displayed by members of the squadron during the war, but none more so than that of one Lancaster crew member on 1 January 1945. It was an act that was to earn him the Victoria Cross, Britain's highest award for gallantry.

Flight Sergeant George Thompson, a tall Scotsman, was the wireless operator of Lancaster PD377 'WS-U', which took off from Bardney just as daylight was breaking on what was a freezing cold New Year's Day. The Lancaster was skippered by a Kiwi, Flying Officer Harry Denton, and the crew had been with the squadron for three months. They had been one of ten squadron crews who had to cut short their New Year's Eve celebrations the evening before to get a few hours rest before the briefing for the raid.

Flight Sergeant George Thompson was awarded the Victoria Cross in January 1945 while serving with 9 Squadron at Bardney. Single-handedly, he courageously fought a fire aboard his Lancaster to rescue crew colleagues trapped at the rear of the aircraft. Sadly, Thompson later succumbed to his awful injuries. (AHB)

Denton's Lancaster was the first to get airborne from Bardney. The squadron was part of a relatively small force of just a hundred bombers from 5 Group carrying out a daylight attack against one of Bomber Command's notoriously tough targets, the Dortmund-Ems Canal.

The 9 Squadron crews had been specifically briefed to attack the canal near Ladbergen, which had been bombed before but had since been repaired. Having arrived in the target area unscathed, Denton approached the canal at 10,000 feet. The weather was good and the run-in to the target went perfectly but just after releasing their bomb load, shrapnel from a heavy anti-aircraft shell crashed into the fuselage just in front of the mid-upper turret, taking out the aircraft's control lines, intercommunications circuit and hydraulic pipes. A second shell caught the nose compartment, momentarily causing Denton to lose consciousness. A fire soon broke out, fuelled by hydraulic oil, and dense smoke filled the fuselage. Much of the nose compartment had been blown away, allowing air to rush through the fuselage to further fan the flames.

The force of cold air had, however, cleared the smoke and now revealed a scene of utter devastation inside the aircraft. There was a large hole in the fuselage and much of the equipment was badly damaged or alight. Denton had recovered enough to regain control of the aircraft and feather the port inner engine, which had also been on fire. The navigator, Ted Kneebone, had lost all of his charts, blown away by the rush of air, but was otherwise all right. So too was the bomb aimer, Ron Goebel, who had somehow managed to survive the devastation in the nose compartment.

Denton set course for home but behind him in the fuselage, Thompson could see that the gunner in the blazing mid-upper turret, Sergeant Ernie Watts, was unconscious. Without hesitation he made his way down the fuselage into the fire and exploding ammunition, easing his way round the gaping hole in the floor, to reach Watts. Thompson then pulled the gunner from his turret and, edging his way back round the hole in the fuselage floor, carried him away from the flames. Then, with his bare hands, he extinguished the gunner's burning clothing.

During his heroic act Thompson had sustained serious burns to his face, hands and legs. He then noticed the rear turret was also on fire. Despite his own severe injuries, he painfully moved to the rear of the fuselage where he found the rear gunner, Sergeant Haydn Price, with his clothing alight, and overcome by flames and fumes. For a second time, Thompson braved the flames. With great difficulty, he extricated the helpless gunner and carried him clear. Again, he used his bare hands, already burnt, to beat out flames on his comrade's clothing.

Thompson, although exhausted, still felt his duty was not yet done. He had to report the fate of the crew to the captain and so he made the perilous journey back through the fuselage. So pitiful was Thompson's condition that Denton failed to recognize him. But Thompson's only concern was for the two gunners he had left at the rear of the aircraft.

It took a remarkable effort by Denton, supported by Goebel and the flight engineer, Wilf Hartshorn, to get the bomber back across friendly lines so that a crash landing could be made near a Dutch village. It was only then that Denton could see the full extent of the carnage in the rear of the fuselage. The figure of the charred George Thompson was barely recognizable but the cheery Scot was still alive.

Bardney pictured in 1948. By then the airfield had closed to flying, although the land was retained for military use. It was later used by the Army before it was used as a Thor Intercontinental Ballistic Missile site between 1959 and 1963, after which the airfield closed once again and the land gradually reverted to agriculture. (Author's collection via Ken Delve)

When the aircraft had first been hit, George Thompson might have devoted his efforts to quelling the fire and ensuring his own safety. But he chose instead to go through the fire to rescue his colleagues. Although he would be in no position to hear or heed any order that might be given to abandon the aircraft, Thompson had continuously put his own life in extreme danger to save the lives of others.

Just over three weeks later, on 23 January, George Thompson succumbed to his awful injuries; he was just twenty-four years old. Sadly, Ernie Potts, who Thompson had fought so gallantly to save, never recovered from his injuries and died in hospital. But the other gunner, Haydn Price, owed his life to the extreme courage of George Thompson. On 20 February came the official announcement of the award of the Victoria Cross to Thompson. It is a remarkable story of self-sacrifice.

189 Squadron returned to Bardney for the final days of the war and would be its last occupants after 9 Squadron's close association with the airfield finally ended in July 1945 when the squadron moved to Waddington. 189 Squadron left in October and disbanded the following month, after which Bardney closed to flying, although the land was retained and used by the Army for storing vehicles. The airfield was used briefly for private flying during the 1950s and then became a Thor Intercontinental Ballistic Missile site between 1959 and 1963. But after the missiles left, the airfield closed once again and the land gradually reverted to agriculture, although a number of buildings remained.

The memorial to 9 Squadron can be found on the village green in the centre of Bardney. (Author)

The site of the former airfield can be found just over a mile to the north-east of the village of Bardney, in the area between Scotgrove Wood (marking the western boundary of the former airfield), the B1202 Wragby Road (marking the northern edge), Austacre Wood (eastern boundary) and the north-western side of Henry Lane running towards New Park Wood (the southern boundary). The southern part of the former airfield can be reached by taking Henry Lane in a north-easterly direction out of Bardney village, or the northerly part by taking the B1202 northwards from the village towards Wragby.

On the village green in Bardney is a three-bladed propeller and spinner as a lasting memorial to 9 Squadron. It has a plaque with the squadron crest and is mounted on stone from the Kåfjord in Norway. The memorial was dedicated in 1980 and moved to its current position in 1992. It stands as a tribute to the squadron and the role of the Norwegians during the famous attacks against the *Tirpitz* during 1944.

Summary of Bardney during the Second World War

Squadron	Date	Aircraft type
9 Squadron	14 April 1943–5 July 1945	Lancaster I/III
227 Squadron	7–20 October 1944	Lancaster I/III
189 Squadron	15 October–1 November 1944	Lancaster I/III
	8 April–14 October 1945	Lancaster I/III

CHAPTER SIXTEEN

Coningsby

There can be no other RAF station quite like Coningsby. As home to the RAF's latest combat aircraft, the Typhoon, and the historic aircraft of the Battle of Britain Memorial Flight, including Lancaster PA474, Coningsby offers aviation enthusiasts and casual observers alike the chance to see past and present come together on a daily basis.

While Coningsby has been associated in more recent years as a front-line fighter base, it was developed as a bomber airfield and spent most of its early history as such, and is now just one of Lincolnshire's three former wartime Bomber Command airfields still in service with the RAF (the others being Scampton and Waddington).

As part of Bomber Command's expansion during the mid-late 1930s, work on developing the land began as early as 1937 but it was not until November 1940 that Coningsby opened as an airfield of 5 Group. At that stage the airfield was grass with no hardened runways, although there were two hangars and a myriad of other buildings on the administrative and technical sites.

The first aircraft arrived in February 1941. These were Hampdens of 106 Squadron and the first operations were flown from Coningsby on the night of 1/2 March when a handful of the squadron's aircraft joined a mixed raiding force of more than 130 aircraft – Blenheims, Hampdens, Wellingtons and Whitleys – tasked with attacking targets in Cologne; all of 106's Hampdens returned safely.

Just days later the larger twin-engine Manchesters of 97 Squadron arrived and the first operations from Coningsby with this type were flown on the night of 8/9 April when three of

Lancasters of 83 Squadron were based at Coningsby for the last year of the war. (AHB)

the squadron's aircraft made up part of a force of 160 aircraft to attack Kiel.

But operating the heavier Manchester from a grass airstrip, particularly during the winter of 1941/42, caused problems. In fact drainage, or rather the lack of it, had been one of the main problems during the construction of the airfield and had resulted in the delay of its opening. Furthermore, the Manchester was plagued with problems, particularly from overheating engines, and so it was often left to the Hampdens of 106 Squadron to bear the brunt of operations. Such were the problems with the Manchester that crews of 97 Squadron are known to have flown the Hampdens of their neighbouring squadron on occasional operations during the summer of 1941.

Despite the problems of the Manchester and the experiences suffered by 97 Squadron, 106 began taking delivery of the type in February 1942, although it would only operate the Manchester for less than four months. But the problems of drainage at Coningsby had not gone away and so the squadrons started to use the new satellite airfield at nearby Woodhall Spa.

By now, 97 Squadron had started taking delivery of the new four-engine Lancaster. At that stage of the war, conversion and training on the new type had to be done locally and so the squadron formed its own conversion flight with two Lancasters. It was not long after that 97 moved to Woodhall Spa, although the conversion flight remained at Coningsby for the benefit of 106 Squadron, due to start taking delivery of the Lancaster from the end of April.

It was around this time that a man who was to go on to become a legend in the RAF arrived at Coningsby to take command of 106 Squadron. This was Guy Gibson who, at that time, was Bomber Command's youngest wing commander at the age of just twenty-three and already a holder of the DFC and Bar, and who would go on to command 617 Squadron and lead the legendary raid on the Ruhr dams. The squadron was soon operational with the Lancaster and took part in Bomber Command's first Thousand-Bomber raid against Cologne on the night of 30/31 May.

After eighteen months at Coningsby, 106 Squadron moved out during September 1942 to make way for the contractors as the airfield was to be brought up to the required standard for the prolonged operation of heavy bombers.

Work lasted nearly a year and after major changes to the airfield, including the construction of new concrete runways and additional hangars, Coningsby re-opened in August 1943. The first squadron to operate from the improved airfield was 617 Squadron, which arrived from Scampton at the end of the month.

The squadron was then under the command of 30-year-old George Holden, a highly decorated pilot with a DSO and a DFC and Bar. On the night of 15/16 September 1943, the squadron attacked the Dortmund-Ems canal, a vital route between the industrial Ruhr and northern ports of Germany. It had been bombed frequently before, although previous raids had largely proved unsuccessful and its flak defences had become notorious amongst Bomber Command crews.

The attack carried out by 617 that night failed to breach the canal and cost the squadron five of its eight aircraft taking part in the raid; forty-eight men were killed, including twenty who had survived the squadron's legendary attack against the Ruhr dams earlier that year. Amongst those killed was George Holden. His crew included four of Guy Gibson's crew who had taken part in the attack against the Ruhr dams: the navigator,

Flight Lieutenant Torger Taerum; 25-year-old Flying Officer Fred Spafford, the bomb aimer; the wireless operator, 24-year-old Flying Officer George Deering; and 25-year-old Flight Lieutenant Robert Hutchison, one of the air gunners. Also killed that night was 22-year-old Flight Lieutenant Les Knight, another 'Dambuster', who had breached the dam on the Eder. It had been a disastrous night for the squadron.

After these terrible losses, 617 was rested from operations for a few weeks to give the squadron time to recover. With the loss of Holden, one of the flight commanders, Micky Martin, another to have survived the Dams raid, briefly took the helm until Leonard Cheshire, another legendary wartime pilot, arrived to take over command of the squadron.

Cheshire had just celebrated his twenty-sixth birthday but with a DSO and two Bars and a DFC he was already one of the most experienced pilots in Bomber Command. When appointed station commander of Marston Moor earlier that year, he had been the RAF's youngest group captain at the age of twenty-five. But Cheshire was not content to be away from operations and so he had taken a reduction in rank to wing commander so that he could command 617.

Bombing-up a Lancaster of 83 Squadron. The 8,000 lb high-capacity bomb shown was first used in 1944 against targets such as large and heavily industrialized areas. (AHB)

101

Cheshire had taken command at a difficult time. Not only was the squadron still coming to terms with its losses from the attack on the Dortmund-Ems Canal, but 617 had now been earmarked for a specialist role and so the crews spent the next three months training in advanced high-level bombing techniques.

The early days of 1944 saw 617 exchange places with 619 Squadron at nearby Woodhall Spa from where 617 would continue in its specialist role. Just days later, 619 was joined at Coningsby by 61 Squadron, which made the temporary move from Skellingthorpe. By now Coningsby had been designated 54 Base as part of Bomber Command's re-organization with responsibility for its two satellite airfields at Woodhall Spa and Metheringham.

Both squadrons left Coningsby in April 1944 to be replaced by Lancasters of 83 and 97 Squadrons. These new arrivals had been designated Pathfinder units with responsibility for the precision marking of targets for the main bomber force, and both squadrons would remain at Coningsby for the rest of the war.

On the night of 8/9 June, four Pathfinder Lancasters of 83 Squadron provided the target marking for Bomber Command's first Tallboy attack (see Bomber Command in the Second World War for more about the Tallboy) carried out by nineteen specially modified Lancasters of 617 Squadron at Woodhall Spa. It was just two days after the D-Day landings and the specified target was a railway tunnel near Saumur, just over a hundred miles to the south of the landing beaches. A German Panzer division was moving north towards the Normandy beachhead and was expected to pass through the tunnel. With the Allies struggling to breakout into north-west France, the landing forces were still in a precarious position and so the tunnel had to be destroyed.

The target area was successfully illuminated by flares dropped by 83 Squadron's Pathfinder crews and the Tallboys were dropped with great accuracy. The result was the tunnel was blocked for some considerable time, delaying the Panzer unit, without a single loss to Bomber Command.

While this attack had been a great success, there were, nonetheless, losses from Coningsby during the latter half of 1944 and amongst the most notable was Wing Commander Guy Gibson. After leading the Dams raid in 1943, Gibson had initially gone to the United States with the British Prime Minister,

Winston Churchill, before being posted to the Air Ministry. But he was determined to return to ops and was briefly posted to East Kirkby as a staff officer before arriving at Coningsby for another ground tour at the beginning of August 1944.

While at Coningsby, Gibson managed to grab three more operational sorties before he was allowed to act as Master Bomber for a raid against Rheydt and Mönchengladbach on the evening of 19 September. As there was no Mosquito available at Coningsby, Gibson travelled to nearby Woodhall Spa with Coningsby's station navigation officer, Squadron Leader James Warwick, where the crew were allocated an aircraft belonging to 627 Squadron. But, sadly, they were not to return from the raid (see Woodhall Spa for more about Gibson's last sortie).

The loss of Gibson and Warwick was a tragic blow to Coningsby and another notable casualty during the last months of the war was 43-year-old Group Captain Tony Evans-Evans DFC, the base commander, who was killed on the night of 20/21 February 1945 while flying on operations with 83 Squadron. Coningsby's final operations of the war were flown on the night of 25/26 April 1945 when just over a hundred of 5 Group's Lancasters attacked an oil refinery at Tonsberg in southern Norway. All of Coningsby's aircraft returned safely.

After the war the two squadrons remained at Coningsby for a while, although their Lancasters were replaced by newer Avro Lincolns during 1946. But by the end of the year both squadrons had moved out. Coningsby was then home to Mosquitos but, by early 1950, they, too, had moved. Bomber Command had started receiving American heavy bombers to build up its force and later that year Coningsby received Washington B1s. By 1952 there were four squadrons based at Coningsby. However, their stay was short-lived as by the following year all four squadrons had re-equipped with Canberra bombers, thus bringing Coningsby into the jet age.

In 1954 Coningsby closed for further development and so the Canberras moved out. Two years later the airfield re-opened with just one main runway. For the next five years it was home to three squadrons of Canberras and then three squadrons of the new Avro Vulcan bombers before Coningsby's long association with Bomber Command came to an end in 1964 when the Vulcans moved out and the airfield closed once

Now home to the RAF's latest combat aircraft, the Typhoon, as well as the Battle of Britain Memorial Flight, RAF Coningsby offers the chance to see old and new aircraft operating on a daily basis. This picture was taken in 2015 when E-3Ds were also operating from Coningsby while the runway at their home base of Waddington was being resurfaced. In the foreground is a Hurricane (left) and a Spitfire, while in the distance, on the far side of the buildings, the tails of several Typhoons are just visible. (Author)

more. It was originally intended for Coningsby to be home to the new development aircraft TSR2. However, following the programme's controversial cancellation, the airfield prepared to receive its first McDonnell Douglas F4 Phantom fighter-bombers. From the late 1960s a number of Phantom squadrons were based at Coningsby before the RAF's new air defence aircraft, the Tornado F3, arrived during the mid-1980s. The F3s have long gone and, in 2005, Coningsby became home to the RAF's latest generation of combat aircraft, the Typhoon.

The Battle of Britain Memorial Flight has been based at the airfield since 1976 and every year thousands of enthusiasts visit BBMF's Visitors' Centre, one of the biggest tourist attractions in Lincolnshire. The airfield can be reached by taking the A153 from Sleaford towards Horncastle. On reaching the centre of the village of Coningsby, turn right immediately after the church on the right. Then, at the mini-roundabout, turn left for the main entrance or bear right for BBMF. It must be stressed that only the BBMF Visitors' Centre can be visited without prior arrangement. All other visits to RAF Coningsby require prior permission.

Summary of Coningsby during the Second World War

Squadron	Date	Aircraft type
106 Squadron	23 February 1941–30 September 1942	Hampden/ Manchester/ Lancaster
97 Squadron	10 March 1941–1 March 1942	Manchester/ Lancaster
617 Squadron	30 August 1943–9 January 1944	Lancaster I/III
619 Squadron	9 January–16 April 1944	Lancaster I/III
61 Squadron	1 February–14 April 1944	Lancaster I/III
83 Squadron	18 April 1944–4 October 1946	Lancaster I/III
97 Squadron	18 April 1944–4 November 1946	Lancaster I/III

CHAPTER SEVENTEEN

Dunholme Lodge

Four miles to the north-east of Lincoln, between the A15 and A46, is the site of the former wartime airfield of Dunholme Lodge. The closeness of the airfield to the city boundary, and its proximity to the airfields of Scampton and Ingham, highlights the problems once encountered when operating three bomber airfields in the same area, particularly when considering the dangers involved with recovering large numbers of aircraft at night during the Second World War.

The airfield of Dunholme Lodge first opened during the summer of 1942 but fields developed next to the villages of Welton and Dunholme had been used by Scampton's Hampdens earlier in the war. And it was Scampton's needs that led to those fields being further developed as its satellite, with the new grass airfield taking its name from a large house called Dunholme Lodge, but simply known amongst its personnel as The Lodge.

The first residents at The Lodge were aircraft and crews of 1485 (Bomber) Gunnery Flight, which moved in from Scampton. Initially, there were few facilities at the new airfield and so its personnel had to get used to travelling to and from Scampton for meals and other administrative reasons. But by October 1942 the flight had moved out so that the airfield could be further developed in preparation to receive Lancasters. Three hardened runways were constructed to the standard A-pattern design, with the main runway being orientated south-west to north-east. Additional hangars were built and the site extended to allow an increase in establishment of station personnel.

The airfield re-opened in May 1943 as part of 52 Base, headquartered by Scampton, as an operational sub-station within 5 Group. The first squadron to arrive at the new airfield was 44 Squadron, which moved in from Waddington under

Posing for the camera are a Lancaster crew of 44 Squadron. The squadron operated from Dunholme Lodge during 1943–44. (AHB)

the command of Wing Commander John Nettleton who, as a squadron leader, had been awarded the Victoria Cross for leading the squadron's daring low level raid against Augsburg a year before.

The squadron flew its first operational sorties from The Lodge on the night of 11/12 June. The target was Dusseldorf and the squadron's Lancasters were part of a large raiding force of 783 aircraft; a mix of Lancasters, Halifaxes, Wellingtons, Stirlings and Mosquitos. The raid was considered a success with extensive damage to the city. But just a month later, on the night of 12/13 July, Nettleton's aircraft failed to return from a raid against Turin. He was leading the squadron's fourteen Lancasters involved in the raid that night, but on the way back from bombing the target his aircraft was shot down by a German night fighter over the Channel. There were no survivors. At the time of his death John Nettleton VC was twenty-six.

The winter of 1943/44 was a hard one for those at Dunholme Lodge and a costly one for 44 Squadron. The Battle of Berlin saw the squadron suffer the highest losses within 5 Group and then two more of its aircraft failed to return from the disastrous raid on Nuremberg on the night of 30/31 March 1944.

At that stage the squadron was under the command of Wing Commander Tommy Thompson and since its arrival nearly a year before, 44 had been operating alone from Dunholme Lodge. But the airfield was big enough for the operation of two heavy bomber squadrons and so in April 1944 Lancasters of 619 Squadron arrived under the command of Wing Commander John Jeudwine.

On the night of 21/22 June the two squadrons each suffered the loss of six aircraft during a raid against a synthetic oil plant at Wesselring, near Cologne. It was, in fact, another disastrous night for 5 Group. The group had provided all but five of the raiding force of 133 Lancasters (the other five being from 1 Group), but the combination of accurate flak and German night fighters intercepting the raid accounted for thirty-seven Lancasters lost (27.8 per cent of the attacking force), including the twelve from Dunholme Lodge.

It was not the only bad night for the new arrivals of 619 Squadron and more losses were to follow. On the night of 18/19 July, thirteen of the squadron's aircraft were part of a raiding force of over 250 Lancasters – a mixed force from all of Bomber Command's main heavy-bomber groups – tasked with attacking railway junctions at Aulnoye and Revigny. The latter target was an all-5 Group effort but the attackers were intercepted by German night fighters and twenty-four Lancasters were shot down, five of which were from 619 Squadron; all but two of the thirty-five aircrew were killed.

It had been a hard time for everyone at Dunholme but there were a couple of legendary Lancs that flew with 44 Squadron during its time at The Lodge. One was ED611, 'KM-U Uncle', affectionately known to everyone as 'Uncle Joe', which had been named after the Russian leader Joseph Stalin. The aircraft had first been delivered to the squadron at Waddington just before its move to Dunholme Lodge, and went on to fly forty-four of its eventual total of 120 ops with the squadron before 'Uncle Joe' was transferred back to Waddington. Another squadron Lanc to go on to amass more than a hundred operations was ND578 'KM-Y Yorker', which was delivered in February 1944 and flew its first op to Berlin on the night of 15/16 February. It went on to complete 121 ops by the end of the war, more than half of which were flown during the squadron's time at The Lodge.

Dunholme Lodge had become very busy and the close proximity of other bomber airfields in the surrounding area, particularly Scampton just a couple of miles to the west, meant that something had to change. The airspace over this part of Lincolnshire had simply become too busy and so The Lodge was closed to operational flying in September 1944 with both squadrons having to move out. The airfield was then transferred to 1 Group. Although it was briefly used by 170 Squadron, The Lodge's days as an operational flying station were over. More than a hundred aircraft had been lost while operating from the station.

With the war in Europe over, Dunholme Lodge was briefly used for the resettlement of Polish personnel before their demob from the service, after which the airfield closed in 1947. However, the site was retained, although not for flying. Bloodhound surface-to-air missiles arrived in 1959 during the worrying days of the Cold War and remained until 1964 when the airfield was closed once again.

The site of the former airfield is bordered by the A15 to the west and A46 to the east and can be reached from either direction.

Parts of the former airfield of Dunholme Lodge can still be found today. Here is the southern threshold of the main runway, which ran in a north-westwards direction, which can be found on Horncastle Lane just after turning off the A46 before the village of Dunholme. (Author)

From the A15 northbound, turn right at the crossroads of the A15 and A1500, and the road, called Horncastle Lane, passes through the centre of the former airfield. It runs eastwards and parallel to the north of where the east-west runway once was. Horncastle Lane can also be accessed from the A46 about a mile before reaching the village of Dunholme. This junction marks the south-eastern corner of the former airfield and about a hundred yards along Horncastle Lane, where the lane bends sharply to the right, marks the area where the threshold for the south-east to north-west runway once was; the lane then heads north-westwards along the line of the former runway.

Lincoln Road, which can be found by continuing along the A46 towards the village of Dunholme and about 200 yards past the left turn into Horncastle Lane, marks the eastern boundary of the former airfield. Along Lincoln Road is the area that was once the technical site, now a private farm, and when entering the village of Welton, the William Farr School stands on the former domestic site and marks where the Officers' Mess and Sergeants' Mess once stood. Outside the school is a plaque acknowledging the site of the former airfield and inside are various reminders of the former wartime airfield. The school is also working on a

The head teacher, Andrew Stones (right), and Brian Riley, the curator of the Heritage Centre (far left), with pupils at the entrance to the William Farr School, which stands on the former domestic site of Dunholme Lodge and marks where the Officers' Mess and Sergeants' Mess once stood. (Author)

Heritage Centre but can only be visited with prior permission. In Dunholme's village church (St Chad), which can be found on the old Lincoln to Market Rasen road passing through the village, is a memorial plaque with the badge of 44 Squadron in memory of those who served at Dunholme Lodge between May 1943 and September 1944.

Summary of Dunholme Lodge during the Second World War

Squadron	Date	Aircraft type
44 Squadron	31 May 1943–29 September 1944	Lancaster I/III
619 Squadron	17 April–27 September 1944	Lancaster I/III
170 Squadron	22 October–28 November 1944	Lancaster I/III

CHAPTER EIGHTEEN

East Kirkby

O ne of Lincolnshire's former bomber airfields not to be missed is East Kirkby, home today to the Lincolnshire Aviation Heritage Centre where there is plenty to see for the enthusiast and family visitors alike.

The wartime airfield of East Kirkby was built on farmland lying on the southern edge of the Lincolnshire Wolds. With Bomber Command needing to expand its number of airfields, the decision to develop the land was made in early 1942. A year later, three hardened runways had been laid, the main one running from north-west to south-east, and hangars and many other buildings erected in preparation for the airfield receiving its first aircraft.

East Kirkby opened in August 1943 as an airfield of 5 Group under the command of Group Captain R T Taffe. The first aircraft to arrive were Lancasters of 57 Squadron, which moved in that

Lancasters of 57 Squadron operated at East Kirkby from August 1943 until the end of the war. (AHB)

same month. The new arrivals had been used to the purpose-built pre-war RAF station of Scampton, and so the basic wartime facilities at their new home came as something of a shock. It also came as a shock to the local villagers, as this previously peaceful and quiet part of Lincolnshire had now been woken by the sound of Merlins and the sight of uniforms in the village was something to get used to.

The squadron flew its first operations from East Kirkby on the night of 30/31 August 1943 when its Lancasters formed part of a raiding force of 660 aircraft attacking the city of Mönchengladbach and its borough of Rheydt. The attack was overall a success. Much damage was caused to both areas and there were no losses from East Kirkby.

The build-up at East Kirkby was rapid. The squadron soon had nearly thirty aircraft on its book and the airfield had become home to more than 2,000 personnel. In November 1943 the squadron's B Flight formed the nucleus of 630 Squadron, under the command of a 26-year-old American, Wing Commander Malcolm Crocker, and both squadrons were to remain at East Kirkby until the end of the war.

Malcolm Crocker was already coming to the end of his tour of operations and so it was not long before he handed over command of 630 to Wing Commander John Rollinson. Sadly, though, Rollinson's life was soon to end while leading the squadron in a raid against Berlin on the night of 28/29 January 1944. Crocker's life, too, would also soon be cut short. Having added a Bar to his DFC, he was killed while leading 49 Squadron at Fiskerton.

The two East Kirkby squadrons were fully immersed in the Battle of Berlin and January 1944, in particular, proved to be costly with nine aircraft lost between the two squadrons during the month. Then, on the night of 24/25 March, the last of the raids against the Big City during this campaign, five of East Kirkby's aircraft were amongst forty-four Lancasters that failed to return. And there were to be more losses a week later when four more aircraft failed to return to East Kirkby following Bomber Command's disastrous raid on Nuremberg.

These were hard times for everyone but the worst night for East Kirkby was still to come. Eleven aircraft failed to return from an all-5 Group raid against a synthetic oil plant at Wesselring on the night of 21/22 June. The raiding force of 133 Lancasters and 6 Mosquitos arrived over the target to find it covered in cloud, and not the clear conditions forecast. The Mosquitos were unable to carry out low-level marking as had been planned and so the Lancasters had to bomb blind using their H2S radar. Worst still, German night fighters were covering the area and thirty-seven Lancasters were lost, including the eleven from East Kirkby: six from 57 Squadron and five from 630.

There were to be further losses, too, including 29-year-old Wing Commander Bill Deas, the new commanding officer of 630 Squadron. Deas, a highly decorated pilot with the DSO and a DFC and Bar, was killed during an attack against a German V-weapon storage dump at St-Leu-d'Esserent on the night of 7/8 July. Again it was a mainly 5 Group effort, involving more than 200 Lancasters, but German night fighters engaged the main bombing force. Twenty-nine Lancasters and two of the Pathfinder Mosquitos were lost. Deas was on his sixty-ninth op.

East Kirkby had now been upgraded and designated 55 Base with responsibility for the control of two nearby satellite airfields at Strubby and Spilsby. Throughout the winter of 1944/45, the two squadrons continued the struggle against key enemy targets as the Allies pushed forward into Germany. But with victory in sight, and just days from the end of the war, there was still time for one more disaster at East Kirkby. During the afternoon of 17 April 1945 the Lancasters were being prepared for operations that night when a fire broke out on board one aircraft belonging to 57 Squadron, setting off its bomb load. A series of devastating explosions followed as one fire triggered another. By the time everything had calmed down, six Lancasters had been destroyed and a dozen or more had been badly damaged. Four airmen were killed and sixteen others injured. It would take a week before East Kirkby was again able to mount operations, just in time for the final action of the war when the final ops were flown from the airfield on the night of 25/26 April. During their time at East Kirkby, the two squadrons had participated in more than 200 operations, during which 121 aircraft had failed to return. A further twenty-nine aircraft were lost having crashed after returning from ops or during training flights.

With the war in Europe over, 630 Squadron disbanded. It had existed for a little over eighteen months and East Kirkby had been its only home. But the war in the Far East was still raging and so 57 was joined by the Australians of 460 (RAAF) Squadron in preparation for a move overseas. However, the planned move overseas did not happen and soon after the war in the Far East was over, after which the Australian squadron disbanded.

Unlike so many of Lincolnshire's former wartime airfields, East Kirkby avoided the axe and was retained by the RAF as one of its post-war airfields. The Lancasters of 57 Squadron were replaced by Avro Lincolns, although the squadron moved out in November and the airfield closed to flying. There was a brief period during the winter of 1947/48 when the airfield re-opened but East Kirkby essentially remained closed until the mid-1950s. It was then briefly used by the Americans for air-sea rescue until the airfield closed, once more, in 1958. Although the site was retained by the RAF until 1970, the land gradually reverted back to agriculture and the remaining buildings were converted for business use.

The future of the former wartime airfield looked to be going the same way as many others but East Kirkby lived on through the fantastic efforts of two brothers, Fred and Harold Panton.

East Kirkby is now home to the Lincolnshire Aviation Heritage Centre, a family run museum and one of the county's biggest tourist attractions, which stands as a lasting tribute to the 55,000 men of Bomber Command who lost their lives during the Second World War. Amongst its exhibits is Lancaster NX611, affectionately known as 'Just Jane'. (Author)

They had grown up near the airfield during the war and had always remembered the familiar sound of the Lancasters operating from the base. They also had a great personal interest in Bomber Command as their elder brother, Christopher, a Halifax flight engineer, had been killed on the Nuremberg raid on the night of 30/31 March 1944. Part of the airfield was bought and some of the old buildings, including the air traffic control tower, restored, and in 1988 the Lincolnshire Aviation Heritage Centre opened. Sadly, Fred Panton died in 2013 but the Heritage Centre, dedicated as a memorial to Bomber Command, lives on, and is today one of Lincolnshire's top tourist attractions.

The former airfield can be reached by taking the A155 from Coningsby to Spilsby. The Heritage Centre is signposted at the village of East Kirkby. At the main entrance, where the guardroom once stood, is a memorial stone to 57 and 630 Squadrons. It was dedicated in 1979 and features a Lancaster in plan form engraved at the top of the stone and surrounded by a low fence with a Lancaster at the front and with the badges of the two squadrons. It commemorates those who gave their lives with the two squadrons during the Second World War. On the left of the memorial is a plaque with a poem titled 'Old Airfield' written by a former member of 630 Squadron, while on the right of the stone is a plaque with words paying tribute to

A memorial stone to 57 and 630 Squadrons stands at the entrance to East Kirkby, where the guardroom once stood. (Author)

the people of East Kirkby who made the squadrons so welcome during the period August 1943 to April 1945, a time when more than a thousand aircrew went missing while operating from the airfield.

The main attraction at East Kirkby today is Lancaster NX611 'Just Jane', which has been maintained in a magnificent condition and carries out taxying rides at specified times. But it is not only 'Just Jane' that is worth seeing. There are a number of events held throughout the year as well as exhibits, memorial plaques, commemorative scrolls and displays to be seen at the centre. There is also a garden of remembrance outside the hangar, and a number of trees planted in memory of various people and organizations. There is so much to see and a visit is highly recommended.

Summary of East Kirkby during the Second World War

Squadron	Date	Aircraft type
57 Squadron	28 August 1943–25 November 1945	Lancaster I/III
630 Squadron	15 November 1943–18 July 1945	Lancaster I/III

CHAPTER NINETEEN

Fiskerton

Five miles to the east of Lincoln, between the villages of Reepham and Fiskerton, is the site of the former wartime airfield of Fiskerton. As with many Bomber Command airfields, it was developed during early 1942 to the standard A-pattern design, with three hardened runways, and first opened in January 1943 as part of 5 Group and a satellite of Scampton.

By the time Fiskerton opened, the first of its personnel had already moved in during late 1942 but the first aircraft did not arrive until early in the New Year. These were Lancasters of 49 Squadron, under the command of Wing Commander Leonard Slee. It was the first wartime move for the squadron as it had been based at Scampton since 1938 and had been at the forefront of operations since the outbreak of the Second World War.

For the best part of the next two years the squadron would operate alone from Fiskerton. The following month the squadron was taken over by Wing Commander Peter Johnson. He would remain in command at Fiskerton for much of the year until his operational tour was complete, after which he was promoted and posted to Woodhall Spa as station commander.

On the night of 17/18 August 1943 the squadron sent twelve aircraft to attack the German V-weapon research establishment at Peenemünde on the Baltic coast where V2 rockets were being built and tested. It was one of Bomber Command's most important raids at that stage of the war and a total force of nearly 600 Lancasters, including those from Fiskerton, were sent to destroy one of Hitler's most secret and important facilities.

Although one of Fiskerton's aircraft had to turn back because of a technical problem, the remaining eleven pressed on to the target. Conditions were good and there was a bright moon that

Fiskerton pictured in 1944. (Author's collection via Ken Delve)

night to increase the chances of success and for the first time a
Master Bomber had been allocated for the raid to help ensure that
the bombing of such a small target was precise. For 49's crews
taking part in the raid, all had gone well up until reaching the
target. Bombs were dropped as planned but as the aircraft were
heading for home they were intercepted by a number of German
night fighters. Amongst Bomber Command's forty aircraft lost
that night were twenty-three Lancasters, of which four were
from 49 Squadron. Only five men from those crews survived.
Amongst those killed was 27-year-old Squadron Leader Richard
Todd-White, one of the flight commanders, whose crew were on
their second operational tour.

There was a brief period during the autumn of 1943 when
the squadron moved out to Dunholme Lodge so that repairs
to Fiskerton's runways could be carried out. Fiskerton had
also been selected to be one of Lincolnshire's airfields to be
installed with FIDO (see Ludford Magna for a description of
FIDO).

Once back at Fiskerton, 49 Squadron became heavily involved
in the Battle of Berlin during the winter of 1943/44. The squadron
mounted nearly 300 sorties against the Big City but lost just

seven aircraft, the fewest losses by any bomber squadron during what had otherwise been a costly campaign.

In May the squadron was taken over by Wing Commander Malcolm Crocker, a 26-year-old American with a DFC and Bar, although Crocker would lose his life the following month. Another sad event took place in June 1944 when Kent Stevenson became the first of two BBC war correspondents to die on active service while reporting on an air raid over Germany (the other being Guy Byam who was killed in February 1945). Stevenson was reporting on a raid against a synthetic oil plant at Wesselring, near Cologne, on the night of 21/22 June and the Lancaster he was flying in was one of six squadron aircraft lost from Fiskerton during the raid. It had, in fact, been a disastrous night for Bomber Command, and 5 Group in particular, with thirty-seven of the attacking force of 133 Lancasters lost (including the twelve previously mentioned from Dunholme Lodge) after German night fighters intercepted the raid.

The restructuring of Bomber Command later that year led to Fiskerton being transferred to 1 Group. As 49 Squadron was to remain within 5 Group, the squadron moved to Fulbeck during October 1944. There was also a period during 1944 when Oxfords of 1514 BATF used Fiskerton as its base before the unit disbanded at the end of the year.

Following the departure of 49 and with Fiskerton now part of 1 Group, two of its Lancaster squadrons moved in; 576 Squadron came from Elsham Wolds and 150 Squadron re-formed at Fiskerton having returned from the Mediterranean. However, 150 Squadron's stay was very brief. It moved out to its new home at Hemswell just days later, leaving 576 as Fiskerton's only resident unit until the end of the war.

While operating from Fiskerton during the final months of the war, 576 Squadron took part in most of Bomber Command's major raids. At the end of April and early May 1945 the squadron took part in Operation *Manna*, the dropping of food supplies to the civilian population of Holland, and then Operation *Exodus*, the repatriation of Allied prisoners of war. 576 Squadron then disbanded. Like many of the RAF's last bomber squadrons to have been formed, 576 had been in existence for less than two years.

With hostilities over, Fiskerton was placed on care and maintenance before reverting to its pre-war use of agriculture. However, part of the airfield was retained for military use and from the early 1960s was used by the Royal Observer Corps. For the next thirty years its headquarters operated from an underground operations room until the end of the Cold War saw it closed down.

The former airfield of Fiskerton can be reached by taking the A158 from Lincoln towards Horncastle. After about two miles take a right turn into Kennel Lane towards Reepham and Fiskerton. Having passed through the village of Reepham, the road, called Reepham Road, which then becomes Fiskerton Road, passes through the centre of the old airfield. This road had to be closed during the war for the construction of the airfield. A memorial to 49 and 576 Squadrons can be found along the road on the left, beside the old runway, and before reaching the village of Fiskerton the old Royal Observer Corps building can be seen on the left.

The layout of the airfield is bordered by the villages of Reepham to the north, Fiskerton to the south, Cherry Willingham to the west and agricultural land to the east. In the village church

The former airfield of Fiskerton can be found along the Reepham – Fiskerton road. The road was closed during construction as it passed through the centre of the site. A memorial to 49 and 576 Squadrons can be found beside the old runway. (Author)

(St Clement of Rome) there is a plaque dedicated to the two squadrons – 49 and 576 – which operated from Fiskerton during the Second World War. There is also a copy of the 49 Squadron Roll of Honour in memory of those who died while serving during the Second World War. Please note the church is locked out of service hours.

Summary of Fiskerton during the Second World War

Squadron	Date	Aircraft type
49 Squadron	2 January 1943–15 October 1944	Lancaster I/III
576 Squadron	31 October 1944–13 September 1945	Lancaster I/III
150 Squadron	1–21 November 1944	Lancaster I/III

CHAPTER TWENTY

Fulbeck

The former airfield of Fulbeck was somewhat unique during the Second World War as it was used operationally by both RAF Bomber Command and the United States 9th Army Air Force. But the airfield was first surveyed and then developed as a relief landing ground for aircraft at Cranwell due to the increase in training requirements during the early part of the Second World War. Consequently, it was not built with heavy bomber operations in mind and so was not used as such until the latter months of the war.

Fulbeck first opened in 1940 and various training aircraft operated from the grass airfield until the end of 1941. The decision was then made to further develop the site for operational use by heavy bombers with the plan to use Fulbeck as a satellite for Syerston in Nottinghamshire within the structure of Bomber Command's 5 Group.

By early 1942 all training flying had ceased from the airfield, after which the heavy contractors moved in. Three concrete runways were constructed and three T2 hangars erected. The first heavy aircraft to move in to Fulbeck were Wellingtons, Whitleys and Manchesters of 1485 (Bomber) Gunnery Flight, which arrived from Dunholme Lodge during the late autumn of 1942. The airfield was then deemed suitable for night flying but with no Bomber Command squadrons yet allocated to Fulbeck, the airfield was once again used by training units from nearby Cranwell.

Next to arrive were Airspeed Oxfords of 1506 BATF, which arrived in the spring of 1943 from Waddington, but, in October, Fulbeck was transferred to the United States Army Air Force. It was one of four airfields in southern Lincolnshire allocated to the US 9th Army Air Force (the others being Barkston Heath,

Folkingham and North Witham) for use by its transport aircraft in preparation for the forthcoming Allied landings in north-west Europe.

Fulbeck was designated USAAF Station 488 and soon the first Douglas C-47 Skytrains started to arrive from the United States. On the night of 5/6 June 1944, nearly fifty C-47s took off from Fulbeck to take part in the drop of American paratroopers near the village of St-Mère-Église in Normandy during the early hours of D-Day.

Once the Normandy bridgehead had been secured, the Americans began to move out of Fulbeck. The airfield was suddenly quiet once more with the exception of a few visitors from nearby airfields during the summer of 1944. But then the Americans returned for Operation *Market*, part of the legendary Operation *Market Garden* in September 1944, when nearly a hundred of Fulbeck's C-47s were involved in the dropping of the American 101st Airborne Division to seize and secure bridges in Holland.

By the end of September 1944 the Americans had no further use for Fulbeck and so all units moved out. The airfield was then handed back to the RAF and its facilities were again considered ideal for use by 5 Group and so the Lancasters and crews of 49 Squadron began to arrive from Fiskerton during the following month.

Fulbeck was placed under the administrative control of 56 Base, headquartered at Syerston, and the first bomber operations from Fulbeck took place on the night of 19/20 October 1944. The target was Nuremberg and was an all-5 Group effort, with 49 Squadron helping make up an attacking force of 263 Lancasters. The crews arrived to find the target almost completely hidden by cloud and so the attack was only partially successful. But it had been an important night for Fulbeck.

Two weeks later a second Lancaster squadron arrived at Fulbeck. This was 189 Squadron, which arrived from Bardney, and the following week, on the night of 11/12 November, Fulbeck's two bomber squadrons operated together for the first time. The target was an oil refinery at Harburg, a borough of the city of Hamburg, in northern Germany. It was another all-5 Group effort, although the amount of damage to the oil refinery is not known. But what is known is that the raiding force of 237

Lancasters caused considerable damage to the surrounding industrial and residential areas. One aircraft of 49 Squadron was amongst the seven Lancasters lost in the raid.

In February 1945 the two Fulbeck squadrons were joined by the Automatic Gun Laying Training Flight, which moved in from its former home at Binbrook. The Automatic Gun-Laying Turret was a radar-aimed turret fitted to some Lancasters during the latter half of 1944. Its rather complex system, known as 'Village Inn', was designed to track and fire on an enemy night fighter without the gunner ever seeing the attacker. 49 Squadron had been amongst the first Bomber Command squadrons to be equipped with the turret and so the squadron again became involved in further trials with the AGLT Flight at Fulbeck during the latter stages of the war.

The two Lancaster squadrons operated together from Fulbeck until the final weeks of the war. The first of the two to leave was 189 Squadron, which returned to Bardney in early April 1945, and then, just two weeks later, 49 Squadron left for Syerston. During its short time at the airfield, 49 Squadron had flown on some sixty of Bomber Command's major raids, losing fifteen aircraft, while 189 Squadron had lost sixteen aircraft during its forty or so bombing missions from Fulbeck.

Large sections of the runways and perimeter track at Fulbeck can still be found today, such as this northern section of the perimeter track, although the site of the former airfield is now private land. (Author)

Sadly, though, there was still one tragic tale to come. On the morning of Sunday 22 April 1945, during 49 Squadron's departure from Fulbeck, one of the squadron's Lancasters, PB463 flown by Flying Officer George Elkington, crashed while carrying out a low flypast over the airfield. To carry out low flypasts when a squadron departs an airfield for the last time is not unusual but, unfortunately, on this occasion the aircraft was so low that it clipped the MT (motor transport) shed and plunged into the ground, killing all six on board as well as fifteen airmen on the ground. It was a tragic end to Fulbeck's short time as a bomber airfield.

Fulbeck was retained after the war as a relief landing ground for Cranwell and so it was soon back to business as usual. During the 1950s Fulbeck was also briefly home to a number of aircraft destined for museums, after which the airfield was formally closed. The main runways were dug up during the 1970s, although sections of the perimeter track were kept for use by farm vehicles. Also to have survived were small sections of two of the former runway thresholds.

The site of the former airfield can be found two miles to the west of the village of Fulbeck. It can be reached by taking the A17 from Leadenham towards Newark and after about two

At the entrance to the former airfield, on Stragglethorpe Lane, is a memorial stone dedicated to all those RAF personnel who flew from Fulbeck during the Second World War and never returned. (Author)

miles there is a small crossroads. Take the left turn and pass through the village of Stragglethorpe. The village marks the north-eastern corner of the airfield and the road then passes along the former eastern boundary. The village of Fenton, two miles to the west, marks the western boundary. The land is now privately owned but at the entrance to the former airfield is a memorial stone, mounted on a propeller-shaped base, erected by the Bomber Airfield Society in 1988 and dedicated to all those RAF personnel who flew from Fulbeck during the Second World War and never returned.

Summary of Fulbeck during the Second World War

Squadron	Date	Aircraft type
49 Squadron	16 October 1944–21 April 1945	Lancaster I/III
189 Squadron	2 November 1944–7 April 1945	Lancaster I/III

CHAPTER TWENTY-ONE

Metheringham

Although in existence for only the last two and a half years of the war, the memory of this wartime airfield has lived on though the Metheringham Airfield Visitor Centre, where its volunteers continue to provide a popular attraction for aviation historians and tourists alike.

Work began during 1942 to construct a new airfield near the village of Metheringham. The site had been identified as suitable for development but the 600 acres required was then a mix of agriculture and woodland. It was also different to other sites found suitable in Lincolnshire because the airfield was to be built in the Lincolnshire Fens, on land that was generally considered unsuitable for heavy bomber operations.

Nonetheless, work was carried out and in October 1943 Metheringham opened as one of a number of new airfields allocated to 5 Group. The airfield had been built to the standard Class A specification with three concrete runways; the main runway was aligned in an almost north–south direction. Although work was far from complete, enough had been done for the first Lancasters of 106 Squadron to move in during the following month.

Metheringham was to be the squadron's home for the rest of the war and the men of 106 Squadron were to be the airfield's only residents. At that time Bomber Command was locked into the Battle of Berlin and from their new home the 106 crews continued the night bombing offensive deep into the heart of Germany. Fortunately, the squadron's early operations against the Big City saw all aircraft return safely, although the squadron's luck would inevitably run out. Nonetheless, its losses of just eight aircraft during what had otherwise been a costly campaign

Sergeant Norman Jackson was awarded the Victoria Cross in April 1944 while serving with 106 Squadron at Metheringham. His story of courage while attempting to fight a fire on the upper surface of the wing, between the fuselage and inner engine, is quite extraordinary. (AHB)

for Bomber Command were far fewer than most other 5 Group squadrons had suffered.

However, the squadron then lost four of its seventeen aircraft taking part in the raid against Nuremberg on the night of 30/31 March 1944. Three of those fell to German night fighters, probably before they had even reached the target, with the loss of all twenty-one men. The fourth crash-landed back in England and the crew survived. But even that crew would soon be lost on operations. Just six weeks later, Flying Officer Dickie Penman and his crew failed to return from a raid on a seaplane base near the French Atlantic port of Brest.

Facilities at Metheringham were never great and its remoteness out on the Fens, seemingly miles from anywhere, meant that conditions were quite harsh during the winter months. Because the airfield was prone to fog and mist forming across the Fens, Metheringham was one of a number of Lincolnshire's airfields to be installed with FIDO (see Ludford Magna for a description of FIDO).

Metheringham will always have its place in Bomber Command's history because of the quite extraordinary courage of a young flight engineer on the night of 26/27 April 1944 during a raid against Schweinfurt. That man was 24-year-old Sergeant Norman Jackson, a former engine fitter from the ranks. Jackson had volunteered for flying duties in 1942 and after training joined 106 Squadron, then at Syerston, at the end of July 1943. He had then moved to Metheringham with the rest of the squadron during late November.

Like so many stories of courage and fate, Jackson need not have been on the Schweinfurt raid that night in April 1944. Earlier in his operational tour he had volunteered to fly an additional sortie with another crew when they had been short of a flight engineer, and so Jackson had already completed his thirty ops two nights before the Schweinfurt raid. But for his own crew, skippered by a Canadian, Sergeant Fred Miffin, Schweinfurt was to be the crew's thirtieth and final op of their tour. The crew had also volunteered to stay together for a further tour with the Pathfinders, and so Jackson had naturally agreed to fly on their final sortie with 106.

Schweinfurt was a long way, a thousand-mile round trip, with the route taking the bombers through some of the most heavily defended parts of Germany. Late in the evening of 26 April, Miffin and his crew got airborne from Metheringham in ME669 'ZN-O'. It soon became apparent there was a stronger than forecast headwind, slowing the aircraft down, which was also proving a problem for the rest of the attacking force.

Not only did the wind slow progress down but it also caused the main force to become scattered, and so by the time Miffin arrived over the target, he could see no other aircraft. They were seemingly all alone. But, fortunately, they found the flak to be surprisingly light and having released their bombs, Miffin turned for home. But no sooner had the aircraft turned to climb away at around 20,000 feet, the wireless operator, Flight Sergeant E Sandelands, informed the crew that a 'blip' had been detected on the aircraft's 'Fishpond' receiver, signalling an enemy night fighter was close-by somewhere to their rear.

Miffin immediately took evasive action by putting the aircraft into a corkscrew manoeuvre: a manoeuvre taught to try and shake off an attacker. Almost simultaneously, the two air gunners, Sergeant W Smith and Flight Sergeant Hugh Johnson, spotted what looked like a night fighter. But it was already too late. The enemy Focke Wulf FW 190 was seen to be breaking away just as its cannon shells riddled the fuselage.

The Lancaster had sustained many hits, particularly in the starboard inner engine. A fire had started near the fuel tank on the upper surface of the wing, between the fuselage and engine, and it was now in danger of exploding.

Jackson had been thrown to the floor during the attack and was wounded in his right leg and shoulder, but despite his pain he decided to fight the fire. He clipped on his parachute, pushed a hand-held fire extinguisher into the top of his battledress jacket, jettisoned the escape hatch above the pilot's head and started to climb out of the cockpit, the idea being that he would make his way back along the fuselage and onto the starboard wing. He then pulled the ripcord of his parachute so that two of his colleagues, Flight Sergeant Maurice Toft and Flying Officer F L Higgins, could hang on to the cords and feed the rigging lines and canopy out of the aircraft. Should anything happen, and Jackson was unable to hang on to the aircraft, the parachute would be released so that it would fully deploy in the aircraft's slipstream and Jackson would descend safely to the ground.

Undeterred by the extreme danger he faced, Jackson continued. His colleagues gathered the parachute together and held on to the rigging lines, paying them out as Jackson squeezed out of the escape hatch and crawled aft. With the Lancaster flying at around 200 mph, the rush of the air meant that progress was hard and slow. Spreading himself as best he could, and hanging on to anything he could, Jackson lowered himself until his feet finally reached the wing. The fire was still raging but, somehow, Jackson managed to spread himself across the wing, with his head in line with the leading edge.

Hanging on desperately to the engine's air intake by just his left hand, Jackson removed the fire extinguisher from his battledress and discharged it into the fire. Remarkably, it seemed to work and the fire started to die down, but Jackson's face and hands were already severely burned. Then, as he struggled to move back towards the fuselage, the night fighter suddenly returned.

Miffin had been able to hold the aircraft steady while Jackson was outside but now he had no option other than to turn away in a desperate attempt to avoid the fighter. With the sudden movement of the aircraft, Jackson was unable to hold on and was swept through the flames, over the trailing edge of the wing, with his parachute dragging behind. When last seen, the

The brick memorial to 106 Squadron, built in the style of an old fireplace, can be found on the former perimeter track at Metheringham. (Author)

chute was only partially inflated and was burning in a number of places.

Had his idea have gone to plan, Jackson should have been thrown clear of the aircraft but he came to a sudden halt. He was still attached to the aircraft by his rigging lines and was now left dangling behind the rear turret.

Realizing the fire could not be controlled, Miffin gave the order to abandon the aircraft. Toft and Higgins had been frantically feeding out the rigging lines and canopy of Jackson's parachute, but they both managed to get out of the aircraft and were later taken as prisoners of war. Also taken prisoner were Sandelands and Smith but Fred Miffin and Hugh Johnson died in the aircraft.

As for Norman Jackson, he had a miraculous escape. He had been thrown clear of the aircraft and despite his horrific injuries survived the descent, even though part of his parachute had been on fire. As daylight broke he managed to crawl to a nearby village where he was taken as a prisoner of war. He was in a pitiful state, but after several months in hospital, he made a good recovery. It was only after the repatriation of the surviving members of his crew that the story of his bravery in trying to fight the fire was told, and soon after came the announcement of the award of the Victoria Cross to Norman Jackson. Few, if any, VCs could have been more gallantly earned.

During the latter months of the war Metheringham was also home to Spitfires and Martinets of 1690 BDTF, which moved in during late 1944 to provide fighter affiliation training for the bomber crews of 5 Group.

The last operational sorties were flown from Metheringham on the night of 25/26 April 1945 when 106 Squadron provided fourteen aircraft for a 5 Group force of more than a hundred Lancasters tasked with attacking an oil refinery at Tonsberg in Southern Norway. It was the last raid by heavy bombers of the war and all of 106's aircraft returned safely.

With hostilities over, Metheringham was briefly home to two other Lancaster squadrons, both in the process of disbanding before, in February 1946, it was 106 Squadron's turn to disband. The airfield was then closed and the land reverted to agriculture.

The site of the former airfield and Visitor Centre can be reached by taking the B1189 Moor Lane from the village of Metheringham towards Billinghay. Having crossed the railway line just outside the village, the road bears a sharp right and then follows the western boundary of the former airfield.

The Metheringham Airfield Visitor Centre, which can be found just off the B1189 to the south-east of the village, is run by volunteers and dedicated to preserving the memory of this former wartime airfield. (Author)

Turning left off the B1189 takes you onto the former airfield and along the former runway to the perimeter track where there is a memorial to 106 Squadron, while continuing along the B1189 takes you towards the Visitors' Centre. It is signposted to the right, opposite the B1191 turn towards the village of Martin. The Centre is managed by volunteers and is open to the public at weekends and on Wednesdays from the last weekend in March (or Easter, whichever is the sooner) until October. Outside the centre is a brick pillar with an imaginative arrangement of a Merlin engine, showing various component parts, on top, which is dedicated to airmen of 106 Squadron who were prisoners of war; an accompanying roll of the squadron's evaders and escapers is inside the Centre. Also outside the Centre is a memorial garden and some original airfield buildings, as well as other items of interest. It is well worth a visit.

Summary of Metheringham during the Second World War

Squadron	Date	Aircraft type
106 Squadron	11 November 1943–18 February 1946	Lancaster I/III

CHAPTER TWENTY-TWO

Scampton

The Dams raid by 617 Squadron, the legendary Dambusters, in May 1943 made Scampton a household name overnight. But few may know that three Victoria Crosses were won from the airfield during the Second World War, or that one man was uniquely decorated with two gallantry awards for separate acts of bravery during the same mission. And so there are many reasons why this historic airfield has rightfully taken its place in the history of the RAF.

Life began for the airfield in 1916 under its original name of Brattleby (also known as Brattleby Cliff), when it first opened as a training aerodrome of the Royal Flying Corps. At the end of

Hampdens and crews of 49 Squadron at Scampton pictured during the early period of the war. (via the Lincolnshire Echo)

the First World War training ceased almost immediately and the airfield soon closed. But the former site was surveyed during the mid-1930s as part of the RAF's expansion plans and the land found suitable for development. The land was then purchased and the contractors moved in to develop a grass airfield on the former site and, in 1936, the new airfield of Scampton opened as a bomber airfield, initially as part of 3 Group, Bomber Command.

The new airfield included many hangars and buildings, both technical and domestic, but many of the personnel first to arrive were accommodated in tents. During the years leading up to the Second World War, Scampton was home to a number of squadrons, operating several types of aircraft, including Handley Page Heyfords, Vickers Virginias, Handley Page Harrows, Hawker Audaxes, Vickers Wellesleys, Hawker Harts and Handley Page Hampdens.

By the time war broke out, Scampton had been transferred to 5 Group with two Hampden squadrons in residence; 49 and 83. Much work had been carried out during the past year or so, with the temporary wooden huts having been replaced by permanent buildings. But despite having two 'C' type hangars and so-called 'permanent' buildings, Scampton was still a grass airfield.

On the opening day of hostilities, the Hampdens were armed and ready to commence operations. For most of the day they remained on the ground but during the early evening six aircraft of 83 Squadron and three from 49 Squadron, led by Squadron Leader L S Smith, took off for an armed reconnaissance over the North Sea to look for enemy shipping. All the aircraft later returned having found nothing.

For the opening months of the war, the two squadrons were able to contribute little to the war effort, their operations being restricted to minelaying, reconnaissance or leaflet-dropping duties. Among 83 Squadron's pilots to have taken part in the first sorties of the war were Flying Officers Rod Learoyd and Guy Gibson, both of whom would go on to win VCs while flying from Scampton later in the war.

There was a brief period in March 1940 when Scampton was home to Fairey Battles of 98 Squadron but by the end of the month the squadron had moved out. As the war progressed, the Hampdens became more involved in minelaying operations and this, for a while, was the principal task, but the squadrons were soon taking part in more offensive operations, such as carrying out attacks against industrial targets and German warships.

On the night of 12/13 August 1940, eleven of Scampton's Hampdens, six from 49 and five from 83, were tasked with attacking the Dortmund-Ems Canal, a heavily defended and vital waterway in Germany. The attack was to be carried out at low level and would hit the canal at a point to the north of Münster where the canal crosses the River Ems by means of an old aqueduct. It was important to destroy this vital artery in Germany's inland-waterway system but because the aqueduct had been attacked before, German defences at the canal had recently been reinforced by additional anti-aircraft guns.

During the early evening of 12 August the crews were briefed at Scampton. Four Hampdens were to carry out diversionary attacks against other targets in the locality while the rest were to attack the aqueduct with special high-explosive canister bombs, each fitted with delayed fuses, and dropped at two-minute intervals. Because of the delayed fuses, timing would be crucial to the success of the operation. Each aircraft was given a precise time to be on target so that it would not be caught in the blast from any earlier weapons dropped.

Led by Squadron Leader 'Jamie' Pitcairn-Hill of 83 Squadron, the Hampdens took off from Scampton around 8 pm, about three hours before they were due on target. As things turned out, the four diversionary Hampdens carried out their attacks but two of the seven aircraft tasked with attacking the aqueduct could not find their target and so bombed Texel Island instead. The remaining five Hampdens arrived in the target area ahead of schedule and so had some minutes to spare.

Conditions were good. The moon was reflecting enough off the canal to aid the run-in towards the target and after circling the area for nearly ten minutes, waiting for the briefed time to attack, Pitcairn-Hill ran in towards the aqueduct. Running in at just 100 feet, the Hampden immediately came under intense anti-aircraft fire from the well-positioned flak guns along both edges of the canal. But despite the wall of flak, Pitcairn-Hill pressed on to complete his attack, releasing his bombs at the right point before swiftly breaking away towards safety.

The second aircraft, flown by an Australian of 83 Squadron, 26-year-old Flying Officer Ellis Ross, then ran in towards the target. His aircraft was seen to receive a direct hit and crashed in flames alongside the canal. The third to run the gauntlet of flak was another Australian from 83, Flying Officer A R Mulligan. Again faced with a wall of anti-aircraft fire, he pressed on bravely towards the target. But his aircraft was hit several times in the port engine, causing it to burst into flames. Quickly jettisoning his bombs, Mulligan then pulled the aircraft up steeply. As soon as there was enough height, he ordered his crew to bale out; remarkably, all four survived to be taken as prisoners of war. The fourth Hampden, flown by Pilot Officer Matthews, was already running in and successfully bombed the target before heading for home on just one engine. It was then the turn of the fifth and last Hampden, flown by 27-year-old Flight Lieutenant Rod Learoyd of 49 Squadron, to make its attack.

Flying Hampden P4403 'EA-M', Learoyd was an experienced bomber pilot with more than twenty operational sorties under his belt. Flying with him that night were his three crew members – Pilot Officer John Lewis, the observer/bomb aimer, Sergeant J Ellis, the wireless operator/dorsal air gunner, and the ventral gunner, LAC Rich.

Flight Lieutenant Rod Learoyd, a pilot serving with 49 Squadron, was awarded the Victoria Cross for his courage while attacking the Dortmund-Ems Canal on the night of 12/13 August 1940. Learoyd's award was the first of eight bomber VCs won by Lincolnshire's airmen during the Second World War, three of which were awarded to men from Scampton. (AHB)

Descending down to 150 feet, Learoyd began his run-in from his holding position three miles to the north of the aqueduct. The defences were now fully alert and familiar with the direction of attack. Flying straight and level, Learoyd pressed on in spite of the intense flak and blinding searchlights. His aircraft was twice hit by anti-aircraft fire, the shells passing through his starboard wing, and by machine gun fire along the underside of the fuselage. Barely able to see because of the glare of searchlights, as well as the wall of flak, he pressed on, aided by John Lewis's commentary. Then, exactly at the right point, the bombs were released and Learoyd turned hard away.

Once clear of immediate danger, Learoyd assessed the situation. His biggest concern was the ruptured hydraulic system, the result of flak damage to his aircraft; this would make landing back at base difficult. But after nursing the shattered bomber back to Scampton he eventually arrived overhead the airfield. It was the early hours of the morning and still dark, and with no hydraulics for the undercarriage and flaps, Learoyd decided to circle the airfield and wait for first light rather than to attempt a crash-landing in the dark. Then, with just enough light to make an emergency landing, Learoyd skilfully sat the Hampden down on the runway. It was just before 5 am.

Post-raid intelligence showed the target had been destroyed. For his leadership of the raid, Jamie Pitcairn-Hill was awarded the DSO while Mulligan, then a prisoner of war, was awarded a Bar to the DFC he had won earlier in the war. But it was Learoyd's attack against the heavily defended target and well alerted defences that had probably been the most hazardous of the operation and, on 20 August, came the announcement that Rod Learoyd was awarded the Victoria Cross. It was the first VC to be awarded to a member of Bomber Command.

Remarkably, just a few weeks later, Scampton was home to a second VC. This time Britain's highest award for gallantry went to a young Scot, 18-year-old Sergeant John Hannah, a wireless operator/air gunner of 83 Squadron, for his extraordinary bravery during a raid against German invasion barges in the port of Antwerp on the night of 15/16 September.

The Battle of Britain was at its height and the Germans were using the Channel ports in preparation for a seaborne invasion of southern England. Fifteen aircraft took part in what was the squadron's largest effort to date. The Hampdens took off from Scampton late in the evening. Hannah was in P1355, skippered by a Canadian pilot, 26-year-old Pilot Officer Clare Connor. Also on board were Sergeant D A E Hayhurst, an experienced observer/bomb aimer with nearly forty operations behind him, and another gunner, Sergeant George James, on his tenth op.

After an uneventful transit to the target area, the flak suddenly opened up as the Hampdens coasted-in at Antwerp. Searchlights were glaring but the moon reflecting off the water meant that Connor could see the concentration of barges below. Descending to 2,000 feet, he then began the run-in to the target. The anti-aircraft fire was now more intense but still the Hampden pressed on. However, realizing they were not best lined-up on the barges, Connor decided to go round again rather than to waste his bombs.

Running in for a second time, the Hampden was once again subjected to the glare of searchlights and intense barrage of anti-aircraft flak. Then, just as the bombs were released, the Hampden was hit in the bomb bay, immediately enveloping the fuselage in fire and causing unbearable heat and damage inside the aircraft. Hannah could see the floor melting beneath his

The second of Scampton's VC winners was Sergeant John Hannah, an 18-year-old Hampden wireless operator/air gunner serving with 83 Squadron, for his extraordinary bravery during a raid against German invasion barges in the port of Antwerp on the night of 15/16 September 1940. (AHB)

feet and all around him the aircraft's spare ammunition started exploding. Due to the unbearable heat inside the fuselage, the second gunner and navigator baled out, but Hannah, even though he was short of oxygen, set about trying to extinguish the fire, using every means possible to beat back the flames. His face and hands were burned black, his eyes badly swollen and the remains of his flying clothing charred.

Hannah's courage meant that he finally managed to extinguish the fire, after which he helped Connor navigate the crippled and charred Hampden back to base. They eventually landed at Scampton during the early hours of the following morning. It was then that the extent of Hannah's injuries could be seen and he was rushed to hospital. Soon after came the announcement that John Hannah was to be awarded the Victoria Cross; he was the youngest airman to receive the highest award for gallantry. Connor, for his part during the raid, was awarded the DFC but he would be killed in November after ditching in the North Sea following a bombing mission in Norway; his body was later found in a dinghy.

By the early summer of 1941 both Scampton squadrons had increased in size, with a combined total of more than fifty Hampdens operating from the airfield, with the station's establishment having risen to 2,500 personnel. In addition to its VCs, Scampton boasted many brave individual achievements during the Second World War and another example is the story of Sergeant Jimmy Flint, a Hampden pilot serving with 49 Squadron, who was uniquely decorated with two gallantry awards for separate acts of bravery during the same mission.

A pre-war pilot with the RAF, 28-year-old Flint joined 49 Squadron in February 1941. He flew his first operations of the war as a second pilot and observer, but on the night of 5/6 July he was the captain of an all-sergeant crew in one of thirty-nine Hampdens tasked with attacking Osnabrück. Having crossed the Dutch coast at 10,000 feet, Flint's aircraft was picked up by enemy searchlights but despite his best efforts he could not shake them off. Suddenly, cannon shells from an enemy night fighter ripped through his aircraft, causing extensive damage to the bomber. But, determined to get to the target, Flint pressed on.

Overhead Osnabrück they were again coned by searchlights but Flint held the aircraft steady long enough to complete their attack before he dived down to low level and headed for safety. The Hampden had seemingly got away but over the North Sea, and just fifty miles from the English coast, his aircraft was attacked yet again; this time by two night fighters.

Three times the night fighters attacked. The Hampden's port engine was soon on fire and the attacks had all but destroyed the inside of the fuselage. With his crew wounded and with no way of communicating with them, Flint took the aircraft down to sea-level until he was almost clipping the waves in the hope of reaching safety. The night fighters had gone but they were still not safe. The Hampden, flying only on one engine, was now approaching the Norfolk coast but Flint was struggling to maintain height. With no chance of climbing safely over the coastline, he had no choice but to ditch the Hampden into the sea just half a mile from the shore.

Two of the crew managed to escape the sinking aircraft but the dinghy had been shot up. Flint had also got out and it was then that he discovered the navigator was still inside. He then crawled back inside the Hampden and found his badly wounded comrade. The aircraft was filling up with water and sinking but Flint managed to haul his colleague out of the escape hatch. Then, without a dinghy, he supported his navigator as he swam towards the shore. When they were just yards from the beach a soldier appeared and helped drag his wounded colleague to the shore. It was then Flint realized that his air gunner had not made it to safety and he refused to leave the beach until all efforts to find his missing colleague had been exhausted and it was clear that he had been lost.

Sadly, the navigator later succumbed to his wounds but Flint was awarded the DFM for his courage and determination in pressing on during the raid and when his gallant efforts to save his crew became clear he was also awarded the George Medal (GM); his citation concluding, 'This airman displayed great gallantry, fortitude and disregard of personal safety in his efforts to save his helpless navigator.'

In November 1941, 1518 BATF formed at Scampton, a unit equipped with Airspeed Oxfords to teach the art of flying 'blind' recoveries. Then, in December, 83 Squadron began replacing its Hampdens with the Avro Manchester, which was followed by the conversion of 49 Squadron in April 1942 to bring the number of operational Manchester squadrons in Bomber Command to five. During its period of operating Hampdens from Scampton, the two squadrons had together lost more than 150 aircraft.

Manchesters from both squadrons, a total of twenty-nine aircraft, took part in Bomber Command's first Thousand-Bomber raid against Cologne on the night of 30/31 May; three of Scampton's aircraft failed to return. But the Manchester remained in service for only a short period of time. It was plagued with mechanical problems and overheating engines and so 83 Squadron soon began taking delivery of the new four-engine Avro Lancaster, followed, in July, by the conversion of 49 Squadron.

The two squadrons had served side-by-side at Scampton for more than four years and had been through much together since the start of hostilities but, in August 1942, 83 Squadron left to be replaced by 57 Squadron. The new arrivals immediately began taking delivery of Lancasters and were ready to commence operations in mid-October; its first raid was a small all-5 Group effort against Wismar on the night of 12/13 October.

The following month saw the formation of 467 (RAAF) Squadron at Scampton, although the Australians moved out just two weeks later, and during this same period 1661 HCU was also formed at Scampton, although this unit, too, soon moved out.

Changes to Bomber Command's organizational structure meant that from early 1943 Scampton was designated the Headquarters of 5 Group's 52 Base, with the station having control of the nearby satellite airfields at Dunholme Lodge and Fiskerton. Other changes included the departure of Scampton's long-term residents, 49 Squadron, which moved out in January.

For a while 57 was the only resident unit at Scampton but that soon changed in March 1943 when a new squadron, 617 Squadron, was formed to undertake a very special task. It had been estimated that the Ruhr valley, the heart of the Nazi's industrial war machine, consumed around 25 per cent of Germany's water. Two reservoirs, one on the Möhne and the other on the Sorpe, held about three-quarters of the water available in the valley and any breach of their dams would impact on hydro-electricity generation and cause mass destruction in the area through severe flooding. After countless experiments the aeronautical engineer Barnes Wallis concluded that exploding a weapon against the surface of a dam would cause a shock wave capable of weakening the structure and that successive detonations would eventually result in the destruction of the dam. Trials began on a method to deliver such a weapon and further tests determined the amount of explosive required, the result being the construction of a spherical bomb, codenamed 'Upkeep', to be dropped from a very low altitude and designed to bounce across the water to the target. The new weapon was to be delivered by modified Lancasters, with Scampton's new squadron tasked to carry out the raid.

Chosen to lead 617 Squadron, and, therefore, the raid, was 24-year-old Wing Commander Guy Gibson, a highly decorated pilot (DSO and Bar, DFC and Bar) and a veteran of more than 170 operations. After much training, and having taken the moon conditions and water level in the reservoirs into account, the raid was planned for the night of 16/17 May.

The plan for the attack, codenamed Operation *Chastise*, was for nineteen aircraft to attack in three sections. The first section

Wing Commander Guy Gibson and his crew boarding their Lancaster for the daring, and now legendary, attack against the Ruhr Dams on the night of 16/17 May 1943. (AHB)

of nine, led by Gibson, was to attack the Möhne dam and, if successful, would then fly on to attack the Eder. The second section of five would attack the Sorpe dam and the third section, also of five aircraft, would act as a mobile reserve and briefed to attack any of the primary targets should the dams not be breached.

Soon after 9.30 pm on 16 May the first wave took off in three sections of three, Gibson leading in 'AJ-G George'. All went well until crossing the Rhine when one aircraft of the second section, 'B-Baker' flown by 23-year-old Bill Astell, was hit by flak; there were no survivors. The remaining Lancasters pressed on at low level in the dark. Gibson's section arrived unscathed over the Möhne soon after midnight and he was the first to attack. Despite being met by a wall of anti-aircraft fire, Gibson pressed on and released his weapon at exactly the right point. The huge column of water seen rising above the dam gave the crew hope but there had been no breach.

Next to attack was Flight Lieutenant 'Hoppy' Hopgood in 'M-Mother'. During the run-in his aircraft was repeatedly hit by ground fire and the Upkeep released too late. The Lancaster was seen to stagger away from the dam and then blew up; remarkably, though, two of the crew survived.

For the next attack, 'P-Popsie' flown by Flight Lieutenant Micky Martin, Gibson ran alongside Martin's aircraft to draw away some of the enemy fire. Martin successfully ran the gauntlet of fire but his Upkeep was released early and exploded short of the dam. Martin now joined Gibson to escort Squadron Leader 'Dinghy' Young's 'A-Apple'. The three Lancasters thundered in towards the dam as the German defenders threw everything they could at the attackers but despite the intense anti-aircraft fire, Young held his aircraft steady for long enough to complete the attack. His Upkeep was seen to strike the dam with devastating accuracy, causing cascades of water over the parapet, but still there was no breach. The fifth aircraft, 'J-Johnny', flown by Flight Lieutenant Dave Maltby, then ran the gauntlet like the others before, but just as his Upkeep was about to be released, the dam was seen to begin to collapse; the previous attack by Young had delivered the vital blow to breach the dam.

Gibson now instructed Maltby and Martin to head for home while he took the others on to the Eder. It took a while to locate

The success of the Dams raid was noted at the highest level. Here, King George VI views the post-raid aerial reconnaissance photos during his visit to Scampton in the immediate aftermath of the raid. Standing alongside the King is Guy Gibson. (AHB)

the dam but the crews arrived overhead to find it undefended. However, its location made an attack and recovery off-target a most difficult task. The first to attack was 'L-Leather' with Flight Lieutenant Dave Shannon, an Australian, at the controls. His Upkeep was seen to hit the target and may have caused a slight breach. Next to attack was 21-year-old Squadron Leader Henry Maudslay in 'Z-Zebra'. His Upkeep was seen to be released late and it hit the dam without bouncing, exploding on impact and catching the Lancaster full in the blast. Nothing was heard from the crew again. Somehow the aircraft had survived the blast, but it was shot down by flak near the Dutch-German border on its way home; there were no survivors. The last aircraft to attack the Eder dam was 'N-Nut' flown by another Australian, Pilot Officer Les Knight. His Upkeep was delivered with great accuracy and hit the dam. The breach gradually widened before a great tidal wave swept down the valley. With both the Möhne and Eder dams breached, the four remaining Lancasters turned for home.

Of the second wave tasked with attacking the Sorpe dam, two aircraft were forced to return early; 'W-Willie', flown by Flight Lieutenant Les Munro, a New Zealander, was hit by flak, and Pilot Officer Geoff Rice's 'H-Harry' had to return to base after losing its Upkeep when the aircraft clipped the waves while crossing the North Sea on the way to the target. What happened to the two others is unclear but 'E-Easy', flown by Flight Lieutenant Robert Barlow, another Australian, crashed close to the Dutch-German border, while 'K-King' of Pilot Officer Vernon Byers, a Canadian, was shot down by flak off the island of Texel near the Dutch coast. This had left just the lead aircraft, 'T-Tommy', flown by Flight Lieutenant Joe McCarthy, another Canadian, to attack the Sorpe dam alone. Although the dam was hit, there was no breach.

The third wave, led by Pilot Officer Warner Ottley in 'C-Charlie', had also suffered badly on the way to the dams. Ottley's aircraft appears to have blown up having been hit by flak soon after crossing the Rhine; amazingly, the rear gunner was thrown clear and survived to become a prisoner of war. The second aircraft, 'S-Sugar', flown by another Canadian, Pilot Officer Lewis Burpee, was shot down by flak over Holland with no survivors. The last aircraft of all nineteen to get airborne, 'Y-York' flown by Flight Sergeant Cyril Anderson, was forced to return to base with its Upkeep intact due to the rear gun turret being out of action. Anderson had tried to press on but was forced to alter his route to avoid known enemy defences. The large detours, combined with misty conditions that made low level navigation all but impossible, soon led to him falling behind schedule and with the hours of darkness rapidly eroding away, he reluctantly returned to Scampton. And so just two aircraft of the third wave had been left to press on to the dams. One, 'F-Freddie' flown by Flight Sergeant Ken Brown, attacked the Sorpe dam. His Upkeep was seen to hit the dam but there was no breach. The other, 'O-Orange', flown by Flight Sergeant Bill Townsend, attacked the Ennepe dam but without success.

Back at Scampton everyone waited anxiously for the Lancasters to return. The first to arrive were those of Maltby and Martin, and later came Shannon and then Gibson and Knight. But there was no sign of Young's aircraft; it would later be discovered that his Lancaster had been shot down by a German coastal flak battery with the loss of the entire crew. From the second wave, McCarthy's aircraft returned from the Sorpe dam and with daylight now getting close, Brown's aircraft returned from the third wave. The last to land was Townsend. It was 6.15 am.

With two of the dams breached, causing widespread flooding and devastation, Operation *Chastise* was considered a success but the raid had proved costly. Eight of the nineteen Lancasters had failed to return with the loss of fifty-three lives. A total of thirty-four gallantry awards were made to the survivors of the raid including the Victoria Cross to Guy Gibson for leading the raid. The other surviving officer pilots who had carried out their attacks – Knight, McCarthy, Maltby, Martin and Shannon – were all awarded the DSO, while the two non-commissioned pilots, Brown and Townsend, both received the CGM. In addition to the pilots, fourteen DFCs and twelve DFMs were awarded to other crew members of those aircraft that had carried out attacks and who had survived the raid.

After the raid 617 Squadron was temporarily stood down from operations to recover. The success of the raid was acknowledged at the highest level and on 27 May the King visited Scampton to meet those who had taken part.

With the Dams raid over, it was time for the airfield to be upgraded and so both squadrons moved out at the end of August. For the next nine months Scampton underwent major development, including the construction of hardened runways, although it retained its status as Headquarters of 52 Base and maintained control over Dunholme Lodge and Fiskerton.

By July 1944 enough work had been completed on the new runways to resume flying from Scampton. The first aircraft to arrive were Spitfires and Hurricanes of 1690 Beam Defence Training Flight (BDTF), one of several units formed for the bomber groups to develop and practise tactics against fighters. Scampton was then transferred to 1 Group and became 15 Base. 1690 BDTF moved out and 153 Squadron moved in, followed by 1687 BDTF and both these units would remain at Scampton until the end of the war.

The war was now entering its final phase but there were still losses to be suffered. One to fall just a month before the end of hostilities was 29-year-old Wing Commander Francis Powley, the commanding officer of 153 Squadron, who failed to return from a minelaying sortie in a Norwegian fjord and the Kattegat on the night of 4/5 April 1945. Thirty Lancasters had taken part but five failed to return and it is believed that Powley's aircraft was shot down by a night fighter.

153 Squadron was joined for the final days of hostilities by 625 Squadron, which arrived at the beginning of April 1945, with both squadrons taking part in the final major raid of the war against Hitler's 'Eagle's Nest' and the local SS barracks at Berchtesgaden on 25 April. They then took part in Operation *Manna*, the dropping of food supplies in Holland, and Operation *Exodus*, the repatriation of prisoners of war from Europe.

With the war over, 153 and 625 Squadrons soon disbanded but Scampton was retained as one of the RAF's post-war airfields. Its role within Bomber Command had become legendary but it had come at a cost; more than 250 aircraft and crews had been lost while operating from the airfield.

Many different flying units came and went over the next decade but amongst the more interesting visitors during the late

Despite several rounds of post-war cuts, RAF Scampton has survived to this day. Its wonderful Heritage Centre is housed in one of the original wartime hangars and includes the restored office of Guy Gibson. Entry to the centre is free but it can only be visited with prior arrangement. (Author)

1940s were B-29 Superfortresses of an American Bomb Group in what were the early days of the Cold War. By 1955 it had been decided that Scampton was to play a major role in the build-up of the RAF's new V-Force and so the airfield was closed to allow further construction and development to take place. The three runways were replaced by one long runway, the extension of which meant diverting the A15 into a long bow-shape at its eastern end, since adopted into the station crest, and by 1958 Scampton was ready for the first Vulcan squadron to arrive.

That first Vulcan squadron was appropriately 617 Squadron and by 1961 Scampton was home to the first Vulcan B2 Wing, consisting of three squadrons. Throughout the 1960s the huge delta-wing Vulcans graced the skies around Lincoln as part of the Nation's defence during what was the height of the Cold War. Then, in 1968, further changes in RAF structure saw Scampton chosen to be the venue for the disbandment of Bomber Command and the formation of Strike Command.

At its peak during the mid-1970s there were four Vulcan squadrons (including the Operational Conversion Unit) based at Scampton but by 1982 all had been disbanded as the RAF looked to the future. The station's role then became training with the RAF's aerobatics team, the Red Arrows, arriving in 1983 followed by the arrival of the Central Flying School (CFS) the following year. CFS moved out in 1995, as did the Red Arrows, but the Reds returned in 2000 and remain at Scampton to this day.

The entrance to RAF Scampton is on the A15 three miles to the north of Lincoln. As would be expected, there are several reminders of this historic airfield's past. Barrack blocks and other buildings carry the names of VC winners, including Gibson, Learoyd and Hannah. The Scampton Heritage Centre, the main historic attraction on site is a must to visit. It is housed in one of the original wartime hangars and contains over 400 artefacts that will be of interest to all aviation enthusiasts, and includes the restored office of Guy Gibson and the legendary grave of his dog. Entry to the centre is free but can only be accessed by prior arrangement as it means gaining entry to the station.

Summary of Scampton during the Second World War

Squadron	Date	Aircraft type
49 Squadron	March 1938–1 June 1943	Hampden/Manchester/Lancaster
83 Squadron	March 1938–14 August 1942	Hampden/Manchester/Lancaster
98 Squadron	2–18 March 1940	Battle I
57 Squadron	4 September 1942–27 August 1943	Lancaster I/III
467 (RAAF) Squadron	7–24 November 1942	Lancaster 1/III
617 Squadron	21 March–29 August 1943	Lancaster I/III
153 Squadron	15 October 1944–27 September 1945	Lancaster I/III
625 Squadron	5 April–7 October 1945	Lancaster I/III

CHAPTER TWENTY-THREE

Skellingthorpe

On the south-western edge of the city of Lincoln is the large housing complex of the Birchwood and Doddington Park estates, but not all residing there will know that they are living on the site of what was once the former 5 Group wartime airfield of RAF Skellingthorpe, home to 50 and 61 Squadrons.

The airfield was developed around local gravel pits and opened in October 1941 as a satellite of Waddington. The first aircraft arrived the following month. These were Handley Page Hampdens of 50 Squadron, which moved in from nearby Swinderby while it was undergoing redevelopment. Although Swinderby's other Hampden squadron, 455 (RAAF) Squadron, left for Wigsley soon after 50's departure, the Australians are also known to have used Skellingthorpe from time to time during early 1942.

At the time the first operations were flown from Skellingthorpe, the airfield was grass and was surrounded by woods and lakes, giving more the appearance of a vintage airstrip rather than an operational airfield. With the introduction of new and heavier bombers, 50 Squadron soon began its conversion to the ill-fated twin-engine Avro Manchester. The pilots and crews serving with the squadron at the time were required to take a break in their operational tour to convert to the new type, with conversion taking place at Finningley in South Yorkshire.

By April 1942 the squadron had received its first Manchesters with all of its Hampdens having gone by the following month. 50 Squadron's first operation with the Manchester took place on the evening of 8 April, but it was propaganda leaflets that were dropped over Belgium and France, and not bombs. Although the Manchester had the potential to be an outstanding aircraft when it first entered service, it was not long before it was suffering from overheating engines as well as other technical defects and it would soon be withdrawn from operations to be replaced by its legendary 'offspring', the Lancaster.

During its brief period of operations with the Manchester, 50 Squadron took part in Bomber Command's first Thousand-Bomber raid against Cologne on the night of 30/31 May 1942. 5 Group contributed more than 150 aircraft on the night but less than fifty were Manchesters, including those from 50 Squadron at Skellingthorpe.

One of the squadron's young pilots taking part in the raid was Flying Officer Leslie Manser. Only days before he had celebrated his twentieth birthday. He had been with the squadron for nine months and this was his fourteenth 'op', although his operational tour had become stretched because of his conversion from the Hampden to the Manchester, after which he had briefly been used as an instructor before his return to the squadron in April.

By the time of the Cologne raid, Manser was becoming used to the technical problems that were starting to plague the Manchester and limit its ability as a bomber. Having taken off from Skellingthorpe late on 30 May in L7301 'D-Dog', he found that he could not climb above 7,000 feet because of a full bomb

Flying Officer Leslie Manser was posthumously awarded the Victoria Cross while serving with 50 Squadron at Skellingthorpe for his self-sacrifice during Bomber Command's first Thousand-Bomber raid against Cologne on the night of 30/31 May 1942. The gallant young pilot had only just celebrated his twentieth birthday and was the only member of a Manchester crew to be awarded the highest award for gallantry. (AHB)

A Lancaster of 50 Squadron pictured at Skellingthorpe during the hard winter of 1943/44. (via Les Bartlett)

load and overheating engines. He would normally expect to be able to climb to a transit height of around 18,000 feet and so he would have been perfectly justified in aborting the mission, but he decided instead to continue.

Overhead Cologne his aircraft was easily picked up by searchlights and anti-aircraft batteries. But Manser held his aircraft steady throughout the final run-in while his bomb aimer, Flying Officer Richard Barnes, counted him down to the target. Then, just after releasing their bombs, the Manchester was hit.

The rear half of the aircraft had been caught by flak and shrapnel had peppered the fuselage and wings. Manser immediately took the aircraft down to below 1,000 feet to get away from the searchlights and flak. He could then take stock of what had happened. A fire had broken out on board and the fuselage was filled with smoke, and the rear gunner, Sergeant B W Naylor, had been wounded. But having escaped immediate danger, Manser was able to climb the aircraft back to 2,000 feet while his co-pilot, Sergeant Leslie Baveystock, and his wireless operator, Pilot Officer Norman Horsley, went back down the fuselage to assess the damage.

Keeping the Manchester in the air was now proving a problem. The aircraft was unstable and barely controllable but Manser held the aircraft as steady as possible, each minute taking them closer towards safety. But just when it might have appeared the situation could be kept under control, the port engine exploded and in no time at all, flames were enveloping the wing. With the wing fuel tank at great risk of exploding, Manser continued to remain calm in the hope that the fire would go out.

Remarkably, the fire did go out and for a while the bomber pressed on towards home. Manser was determined to get his crew back safely but, flying on just one engine, the Manchester had been gradually losing height. He maintained control for as long as he could but when a crash became inevitable, he ordered the crew to abandon the aircraft. Barnes, Horsley, Naylor and the two other gunners, Sergeants King and Mills, all baled out, leaving just the two pilots at the front of the aircraft.

With the rest of the crew safely away, Baveystock handed Manser his parachute. But Manser waved it away, saying that

The 50 Squadron crew of Mike Beetham pictured at Skellingthorpe during 1944 as their operational tour was coming to an end. Standing L–R: Sergeant Jock Higgins (air gunner), Pilot Officer Johnny Blott DFC (air gunner), Flight Lieutenant Mike Beetham DFC (pilot), Flying Officer Frank Swinyard DFC (navigator), Pilot Officer Les Bartlett DFM (bomb aimer). Sitting L–R: Flight Lieutenant Ted Adamson DFC and Sergeant Reg Payne (wireless operator). (via Les Bartlett)

he could only hold the aircraft steady for a few more seconds. Baveystock made his escape and as the crew descended to safety they saw the aircraft, still with their gallant young captain on board, plunge to earth and burst into flames.

The Manchester had crashed three miles east of the Belgian village of Bree, close to the Dutch border. Apart from Barnes who was injured and taken as a prisoner of war, the rest of the crew evaded capture and returned home to England. It was then that the full story of Manser's heroic sacrifice was told and shortly after came the announcement of the award of the Victoria Cross to Leslie Manser. It was the only time a VC was awarded to a member of a Manchester crew and in a personal letter to Manser's family, Arthur Harris wrote 'no Victoria Cross has been more gallantly earned'.

There were to be two more Thousand-Bomber raids but by the time of the third, against Bremen towards the end of June, 50 Squadron had moved back to Swinderby while contractors moved in to upgrade Skellingthorpe. The new airfield was constructed to the standard bomber design with three concrete

Each squadron at Skellingthorpe boasted a centurion Lancaster and here the station's personnel are seen waving them off during 1944. Nearest the camera is ED860 'QR-N Nuts' of 61 Squadron, which went on to complete 130 missions, and furthest is ED588 'VN-G George', which was eventually lost on the night of 29/30 August 1944 when it failed to return from a raid against Königsberg, believed to be its 128th op. (AHB)

runways; the main running from the B1190 Doddington Road, which had to be closed when aircraft were departing, in a north-easterly direction towards Lincoln Cathedral. The runways were all linked by a perimeter track and there were enough hard standings for two heavy bomber squadrons. One Type B1 hangar and two Type T2s were erected for aircraft maintenance and numerous Nissen huts were situated around the airfield for administrative and domestic purposes.

By October 1942 work was complete and so 50 Squadron, now equipped with Lancasters, moved back to Skellingthorpe, its home for the rest of the war. Although the new runways were occasionally used by other heavy bombers from the many neighbouring airfields around Lincoln, 50 Squadron operated alone from Skellingthorpe until Lancasters of 61 Squadron arrived from Syerston in November 1943. From then on, with the exception of a few weeks in early 1944 when 61 temporarily moved to Coningsby, these two Lancaster squadrons operated together from Skellingthorpe until the end of the war.

61 Squadron had arrived at Skellingthorpe at the start of the Battle of Berlin. It was to be a long and hard campaign against the Big City during the winter of 1943/44 and one that was to cost the squadron eleven aircraft from just over 250 sorties flown against the Nazi capital. Both squadrons then took part in Bomber Command's disastrous raid against Nuremberg on the night of 30/31 March 1944. Four of the ninety-five aircraft that failed to return were from 50 Squadron. One of the squadron's aircraft taking part that night was flown by 20-year-old Flight Lieutenant Michael Beetham (later Marshal of the Royal Air Force Sir Michael Beetham). His bomb aimer, Flight Sergeant Les Bartlett, kept a diary throughout his tour of operations at Skellingthorpe. An extract for that night reads:

We crossed the enemy coast and as we drew level with the south of the Ruhr valley things began to happen. Enemy night fighter flares were all around us and in no time at all several combats were taking place with aircraft going down on both sides. So serious was the situation that I remember looking at the other poor blighters going down and thinking to myself that it must be our turn next. It was just a question of time. We altered course for Nuremberg and I looked down at the area over which we had just flown. It looked like a battlefield, there were kites burning on the deck and bombs going off where they had not jettisoned their load; such a piece of aerial disaster I had not seen before and certainly hope never to see again. On the way to the target the wind became changeable and we almost ran into the defences of Schweinfurt but altered course just in time. We carried out a normal approach to the target and scored direct hits with our 4,000 lb 'Cookie' and our 1,000 lb bombs and incendiaries. We set course for home and eventually landed back at base. Back in debriefing we heard the full story of our squadron's effort; four aircraft lost with another written-off on take-off. It was the worst night for our squadron.

The two Skellingthorpe squadrons continued to take part in Bomber Command's major efforts for the rest of the war, after which they both moved out. For a brief period the airfield was home to two other Lancaster squadrons, but they were both in the process of disbanding. With the Lancasters having gone, the airfield was retained for use as a relief landing ground for Swinderby into the early 1950s, but was then closed. Although much of the airfield remained for many years, it was gradually sold off and developed for housing.

The head teacher, Adrian Jones, and pupils of the Leslie Manser School. The school was built on the former airfield of Skellingthorpe and proudly takes its name from Flying Officer Leslie Manser VC. (Author)

The site of the former airfield is within the city boundary of Lincoln and bordered by the A46 Lincoln bypass to the west, the B1378 Skellingthorpe Road to the north, the B1190 Doddington Road to the south and Hartsholme Park to the east. Due to expansion of the housing estates in the early 1980s, an annex to the Birchwood County Junior School was opened and named the Leslie Manser Primary School as a tribute to the gallant wartime pilot who had been posthumously awarded the Victoria Cross. The school was opened by Leslie's brother, Cyril Manser, and a tribute to Flying Officer Leslie Manser VC stands proudly in the school, which can be found on Kingsdown Road. Outside the Community and Leisure Centre on Birchwood Avenue is a memorial to 50 and 61 Squadrons, which stands in memory of all those who gave their lives while serving with the squadrons during the Second World War. It was unveiled in 1989 by Marshal of the Royal Air Force Sir Michael Beetham GCB CBE DFC AFC who served as a young Lancaster pilot with 50 Squadron during the hard winter of 1943/44. In addition to the memorial, a Casualty Roll of Honour was produced in 1991, listing the 1,972 aircrew and ground personnel killed while serving with the two squadrons during the Second World War, and presented to the City of Lincoln. More memorabilia can be found in the

The former airfield of Skellingthorpe is now a housing estate. The memorial to 50 and 61 Squadrons can be found outside the Leisure Centre on Birchwood Avenue. (Author)

Birchwood Community and Leisure Centre and also next to the memorial is a surviving section of perimeter track.

In the village of Skellingthorpe, outside the Community Centre, is a memorial to RAF Skellingthorpe. Dedicated in 1991, the memorial has the badges of 50 and 61 Squadrons and an inscription of a poem by R W Gilbert set on a semi-circular base of coloured bricks in the form of the RAF roundel and surrounded by a low wall. It was erected by the people of the parish in grateful remembrance of the airmen and airwomen who served at RAF Skellingthorpe during 1941–45. Adjacent to the memorial is the Skellingthorpe Heritage Room, which has an exhibition of photographs relating to the wartime airfield; it is open all year and admission is free.

Summary of Skellingthorpe during the Second World War

Squadron	Date	Aircraft type
50 Squadron	26 November 1941–19 June 1942	Hampden/Manchester/Lancaster
	17 October 1942–14 June 1945	Lancaster I/III
61 Squadron	16 November 1943–31 January 1944	Lancaster I/III
	15 April 1944–15 June 1945	Lancaster I/III

CHAPTER TWENTY-FOUR

Spilsby

L ocated nine miles inland from Skegness on the southern edge of the Lincolnshire Wolds, and about three miles east of the historic market town from where it takes its name, is the site of the former 5 Group airfield of Spilsby.

Built on 630 acres of farmland to the standard A-pattern bomber airfield design, with three concrete runways, Spilsby opened in September 1943 as a satellite of East Kirkby. Lancasters of 207 Squadron moved in the following month, taking advantage of a full moon period to move in when there were few operations being carried out by Bomber Command.

For the previous year the squadron had been settled at Langar in Nottinghamshire, where facilities had been good and 207 had been the only resident squadron. The squadron's personnel had enjoyed sole use of the base and the local facilities. Furthermore, there were fewer airfields in that part of the country and so the quieter airspace meant that operating in and out of their home base had been relatively easy. But things were now going to be very different. With so many airfields in close proximity, and being so close to the North Sea, the move had, to many, come as something of an unwelcome surprise.

For the new arrivals it was to be a long and hard winter in the cold and blustery east Lincolnshire countryside. Facilities at Spilsby were basic. Nissen huts of various sizes provided most, if not all, of the airfield's so-called buildings. Aircraft were dispersed around the airfield and so getting about usually required a bicycle, if one could be acquired, and to make matters worse, the weather that winter seemed to have been wetter than normal and so produced lots of mud.

207 Squadron had arrived at the start of the campaign against Berlin. It would prove to be the hardest campaign of them all,

and for those serving at Spilsby it was to be no different than elsewhere. Raids against the Nazi capital during January 1944 alone resulted in at least seven squadron aircraft failing to return; three were lost in one night at the end of the month. The losses continued and even when the campaign was coming to an end, during the last days of March 1944, 207 lost four more aircraft: two during the final raid against the capital and two during the disastrous raid on Nuremberg on the night of 30/31 March.

Under the reorganization of Bomber Command, Spilsby had become part of 55 Base headquartered by East Kirkby. The squadron was led during this period by Wing Commander John Grey who commanded the squadron with great success and would soon add the DSO to his DFC for his great skill and leadership in action. Spilsby was also home during this period for 5 Group's anti-aircraft school, which opened in May 1944 to train gunners on airfield protection.

207 Squadron was joined at Spilsby at the end of September by the Lancasters of 44 Squadron when 44's former base, Dunholme Lodge, was transferred to 1 Group. The two squadrons then operated side-by-side during the final winter of hostilities before

Unveiled in 2012, the new memorial to RAF Spilsby can be found in Monksthorpe where it sits on the concrete base of the former fire tender shed, close to the bomb dump where an accident in April 1944 cost the lives of ten armourers. (Author)

The obelisk from the original memorial to RAF Spilsby can now be found in the grounds of Monksthorpe Chapel, adjacent to the former airfield. (Author)

they both flew their final operations of the war on 25 April 1945 against Hitler's 'Eagle's Nest and the local SS barracks at Berchtesgaden.

During its wartime existence, nearly a hundred Lancasters had been lost while operating from Spilsby, either on operations or as a result of flying accidents. With the war over, 44 Squadron moved out and was immediately replaced by Lancasters of 75 (New Zealand) Squadron, although this squadron disbanded in October, the same month as 207 Squadron moved out.

Although the flying units had all gone, Spilsby remained open until the end of 1946 before finally being put on care and maintenance. It then remained as an unused airfield until 1955 when it briefly opened again for use by the United States Air Force. But three years later the airfield closed once more, after which the land was sold off for agricultural purposes. Today there are few reminders of the former airfield, although a B1 hangar has survived and is used for storage.

The site of the former airfield can be found to the east of the village of Spilsby and can be reached from the village by turning right off the A16 onto the B1195. After three miles the road passes through the village of Great Steeping and the road then marks the southern boundary of the former airfield. In 2001 a memorial was dedicated to all those who served at RAF

Spilsby between September 1943 and October 1945. But after many years of being exposed to the Lincolnshire weather, the decision was made to replace it with a new memorial. The new memorial was unveiled in 2012 and is sculptured from Portland stone. It comprises three small pillars and a larger one to signify the Morse code dots and dash for the symbolic letter 'V'. It can be found in Monksthorpe and sits on the wartime concrete base of the former fire tender shed, close to the old bomb dump where an accident on Monday 10 April 1944 cost the lives of ten squadron armourers. The obelisk from the original memorial can be found in the grounds of Monksthorpe Chapel, adjacent to the former airfield.

Summary of Spilsby during the Second World War

Squadron	Date	Aircraft type
207 Squadron	12 October 1943–29 October 1945	Lancaster I/III
44 Squadron	30 September 1944–20 July 1945	Lancaster I/III

Chapter Twenty-Five

Spitalgate (Grantham)

Although not home to any bomber squadrons during the Second World War, the airfield of Spitalgate (formerly Grantham) is included for completeness because many types of bomber aircraft flew from the airfield during the build-up to war and also because it provided valuable support to Bomber Command throughout the period of hostilities.

The airfield's history dates back to the First World War when it was first used as a training airfield for the Royal Flying Corps. Then, as a training base in the 1920s, it was one of the busiest airfields in the country and after the formation of Bomber Command in 1936, the airfield became one of 5 Group's main operating bases during the RAF's expansion scheme of the late 1930s.

At that time the airfield was home to two squadrons of Hawker Hinds but they were replaced by Fairey Battles just a year before the outbreak of the Second World War. However, the size of the airfield and the grass runways meant it was not suitable for the larger aircraft types of Bomber Command, and so the station reverted to flying training.

During the early years of the Second World War, the airfield was used by Hawker Harts, Avro Ansons and Hawker Audaxes of 12 Service Flying Training School. In 1942 the school was re-named 12 Advanced Flying Unit for the training of pilots and converted to Blenheims, which it then operated until the end of the war. The airfield was also home to 5 Group Communications Flight, which operated Tutors, Oxfords, Magisters and Proctors from the early part of the war until late 1943, and was also home to 1536 BATF from early 1943 until the end of hostilities.

It was during 1944 that the airfield was officially re-named Spitalgate. Although not an operational station, there was the

Now used by the Army, the former airfield of Spitalgate can easily be seen from the junction of the A52 and B6403 High Dike to the south-east of Grantham. (Author)

occasional damage and losses as a result of attacks by enemy intruders who were often prowling the skies over Lincolnshire in search of RAF bombers returning home from operations.

Although two of its three runways had been covered in Sommerfeld steel tracking, being a grass airfield meant that Spitalgate was never going to be suitable for heavier and more modern aircraft, and so the airfield closed to flying soon after the end of the war.

Unlike many former wartime airfields, Spitalgate was retained by the RAF and used in a non-flying capacity until 1975, after which RAF Spitalgate was transferred to the Army. It was then re-named Prince William of Gloucester Barracks and since 1993 has been the headquarters of The Royal Logistics Corps Territorial Army. It can be found two miles to the south-east of the town of Grantham. The area of the former airfield can still be clearly seen to the north-west of the junction between the A52, which marks the southern boundary, and the B6403 High Dike road, which marks the eastern extremity. Access to the site can only be attained with prior permission.

CHAPTER TWENTY-SIX

Strubby

L ocated just inland to the south-west of Mablethorpe, the airfield of Strubby was one of the last of Lincolnshire's airfields to be opened during the Second World War and the most easterly of the county's airfields of Bomber Command.

As the RAF went in search of even more airfields during the Second World War, a piece of flat and fertile land, soon to become the airfield of Strubby, was identified as suitable for development as a bomber airfield for 5 Group. Work began in 1943 to the standard A-pattern layout, with three hardened runways

Members of 619 Squadron next to Lancaster 'PG-D'. Strubby was the most easterly of Lincolnshire's airfields of Bomber Command and one of the last in the county to be opened during the Second World War. 619 spent the final months of hostilities, including the winter of 1944–45, based at the airfield. (via the Lincolnshire Echo)

surrounded by a perimeter track and aircraft hard standings, with three hangars (one B1 and two T2s) and a technical site on the south-west part of the airfield. Accommodation was dispersed around the airfield with enough space for more than 2,000 personnel.

By April 1944 the airfield was considered ready for operations as a satellite airfield of 55 Base at East Kirkby. But, at that stage, there was no bomber squadron in immediate need of a home and so Strubby was loaned to RAF Coastal Command.

The first aircraft known to have operated from the new airfield were Vickers Warwicks, used for air-sea rescue, and two squadrons of Bristol Beaufighter light bombers operating as a strike wing. However, by September 1944 the airfield was needed by Bomber Command and so the Coastal Command units moved out to make way for the Lancasters of 619 Squadron, which were to remain at Strubby for the final months of the war.

The first Bomber Command operations from Strubby took place on the night of 4/5 October 1944 when five of the squadron's aircraft were part of a small force of less than fifty Lancasters tasked with laying mines off the coast of southern Norway and the Kattegat. One of the two aircraft lost that night was from 619.

619 Squadron operated alone from Strubby until the final days of the war when 227 Squadron arrived. The new arrivals had moved in with the war in its final month and so the two squadrons saw out the final few days of hostilities together.

Fortunately, 619's losses while operating from Strubby during the final phase of the war were few but, even so, it had lost sixty-five aircraft while operating from Strubby, either lost on operations or having crashed elsewhere, and so the squadron had not escaped the war unscathed. It also appears that 619 suffered 5 Group's final loss of the war as one of its Lancasters was one of two aircraft that failed to return from the raid against Hitler's Eagle's Nest and SS barracks at Berchtesgaden on 25 April 1945. The aircraft was flown by a Canadian pilot, Flying Officer Wilf De Marco, and he was killed with three of his crew; 21-year old Pilot Officer Norman Johnston (navigator) and 25-year-old Warrant Officer Gordon Walker (air gunner) were also Canadians, while Sergeant Edward Norman, the young 19-year-old mid-upper gunner, was a local lad from Lincolnshire.

With the war at its end, the two squadrons took part in Operation *Exodus*, the repatriation of prisoners of war, before they both left Strubby to be disbanded. The airfield was then used to build up the ground component of Tiger Force destined for the Far East, but when the war with Japan came to an end the ground units left Strubby, after which the airfield was closed to flying.

Strubby was one of the few bomber airfields in Lincolnshire to survive the post-war axe. The airfield re-opened in 1949 as a satellite for Manby and for more than twenty years many RAF aircraft and units came and went before RAF Strubby closed in 1972, after which the land was sold. While much of the former airfield reverted to agriculture, the north-eastern part was developed as a heliport for the transportation of oil workers to and from the North Sea rigs. When the company relocated to Humberside Airport in 1999, the facilities were retained for use by the Strubby Aviation Club. Just to the south of the club is the Lincolnshire Gliding Club and part of the taxiway near the technical site in the south-western corner of the airfield is used for go-carting.

The former wartime airfield is bounded by several roads. Using directions from the village of Withern, the A157 towards

The site of Strubby today, where a new memorial to all those who served at the station during the period 1944–72 and many former wartime buildings can be found. (Author)

Maltby le Marsh follows the northern boundary of the airfield and then turns sharp right along the eastern boundary, with the gliding club marking the north-eastern extremity. The junction with the A1104 marks the eastern extremity of the former airfield and then following the A1104 towards Beesby takes you along the south-eastern boundary with the southern-most point marked by the junction with the B1373. Turning right along the B1373 (back towards Withern) takes you along the western part of the former airfield. Just before the Woodthorpe Hall Garden Centre is a small turning to the right (to Lincs Aquatics) where many of the airfield's former buildings have survived. There is also a new memorial to RAF Strubby, made of black granite and unveiled in 2014, to commemorate all who served there, in war and peace, between 1944 and 1972.

Summary of Strubby during the Second World War

Squadron	Date	Aircraft type
619 Squadron	28 September 1944–29 June 1945	Lancaster I/III
227 Squadron	5 April–7 June 1945	Lancaster I/III

CHAPTER TWENTY-SEVEN

Swinderby

To the south-west of the city of Lincoln, mid-way along the A46 between Lincoln and Newark, is the former airfield of Swinderby. As a wartime airfield it was part of both 1 and 5 Groups, and so it could appear in either section of this book, but I have included it under 5 Group as that is where it spent most of its time during the war.

Although the land had been identified as suitable for development under the RAF's expansion plans of the late 1930s, progress from there on had been slow and so the airfield was not ready by the outbreak of the Second World War. With the pace of work then stepping up, the all-grass airfield did not take long to complete and Swinderby opened in August 1940.

Swinderby was initially allocated to 1 Group and the first units to arrive were two Polish squadrons of Fairey Battles; 300 (Mazowiecki) and 301 (Pomorski) Squadrons. The first operations were flown from the airfield the following month when the Poles carried out a number of attacks against German invasion barges in the Channel ports of northern France and Belgium. But the Battle was never intended to be one of Bomber Command's main offensive aircraft and so the two Polish squadrons began converting to the Wellington and by the end of the year had begun operations with the new type.

Operating the heavier Wellington from a grass airfield during the winter months was never going to be easy and so when conditions became too bad the squadrons temporarily operated from other airfields nearby, where there were hardened runways and hard standings. Nonetheless, the two Polish squadrons operated together from Swinderby until July 1941 when control of the airfield was passed to 5 Group. The Poles moved out to be

Lancasters of 50 Squadron were based at Swinderby during the summer of 1942. (AHB)

replaced by Hampdens of 50 Squadron and the newly-formed 455 (RAAF) Squadron, the first bomber squadron of the RAAF.

The nucleus of the Australian squadron consisted of men who had joined up together in New South Wales. The squadron had started forming at Swinderby in early June and immediately began working up for operations pending the arrival of more squadron members from Australia. Using Hampdens borrowed from 50 Squadron, 455 flew its first operations of the war on the night of 25/26 August when five of its aircraft joined a force of nearly forty Hampdens, plus a handful of Manchesters, to attack Mannheim in Germany. The raid achieved moderate success and all the squadron's aircraft returned safely.

The Australians were able to use their own aircraft for the first time on the night of 29/30 August when a Hampden flown by Squadron Leader French joined forces with 50 Squadron to help make up a raiding force of nearly 150 bombers to attack Frankfurt. French had already completed a tour of operations with 50 Squadron and had been the first Australian of the war to be awarded the DFC, and the raid against Frankfurt that night marks the first official bombing sortie flown by an Australian squadron during the war. But bad weather over the target area prevented accurate bombing, although French and his crew returned safely.

More Hampdens soon began to arrive and by the end of the year the Australian squadron had increased its establishment to twenty-seven aircraft under the command of 27-year-old Wing Commander Grant Lindeman, a pre-war officer. But the winter that followed was typically bad and like many of Lincolnshire's early bomber airfields, Swinderby's grass runways meant the airfield was not capable of operating the new four-engine heavy bombers now entering service with the RAF. The truth was that Swinderby was badly in need of redevelopment and so both Hampden squadrons moved out.

Having been upgraded, Swinderby's role briefly changed to one of converting new bomber crews to the four-engine Lancaster. Until then, squadrons had been left to manage the conversion of their own crews, usually achieved by each squadron having its own conversion flight, but from now on resources were to be pooled. This decision led to the formation of 1654 HCU in May 1942. The HCU was equipped with a mix of Manchesters and Lancasters, but within a few weeks the HCU had moved out to make way for the return of 50 Squadron, which moved back to Swinderby from Skellingthorpe while the latter went through its own redevelopment for heavy bomber operations.

By the time it returned in June 1942, 50 Squadron was equipped with Manchesters and it began operations almost immediately. But with the Manchester continuing to suffer technical problems, the squadron soon began conversion to the Lancaster as more aircraft became available; 50 Squadron was the sixth Bomber Command squadron to convert to the new type. However, the squadron's return to Swinderby was short-lived and it moved back to Skellingthorpe in October, after which Swinderby ceased to be an operational airfield.

From now on Swinderby would be a training airfield and for the rest of the war was home to 1660 HCU, a training unit made up from the conversion flights of a number of nearby squadrons, equipped with a mix of Stirlings and Halifaxes. With this change in role came the eventual transfer of Swinderby to 7 (Training) Group in 1944, followed by the re-designation of the airfield as 75 Base. At its peak there were anything up to 3,000 aircrew under training at Swinderby. As hostilities came to an end there was no requirement for more trained bomber crews at the front line, and so 1660 HCU disbanded, although the wind-down of training aircrew took several months.

During the late 1940s Swinderby continued to be used as a training base. Over the following years it was home to various flying training schools and entered the jet age during the mid-1950s with the arrival of aircraft such as Vampires and Meteors.

A new memorial, dedicated in 2014 to all those who served at RAF Swinderby from 1940 to 1993, can be found outside the village hall at Witham St Hughs. (Author)

Flying at the airfield continued until 1964 when the role of Swinderby changed to RAF recruit training and by the early 1970s every airman to join the RAF passed through Swinderby. There was also a period when the airfield was home to a number of De Havilland Chipmunk basic trainers, used for flying selection and elementary flying training for new pilots entering the RAF, before RAF Swinderby closed in 1993.

The former airfield is clearly visible from the A46 as the road passes along the entire length of the airfield's north and western boundary. A couple of hangars remain and the domestic site has now been developed as the new village of Witham St Hughs. A memorial at the village hall was dedicated in 2014 to all those who served at Swinderby from 1940 until 1993.

Summary of Swinderby during the Second World War

Squadron	Date	Aircraft type
300 (Mazowiecki) Squadron	22 August 1940–17 July 1941	Battle I / Wellington I
301 (Pomorski) Squadron	28 August 1940–17 July 1941	Battle I / Wellington I
455 (RAAF) Squadron	6 June 1941–7 February 1942	Hampden I
50 Squadron	19 July–25 November 1941	Hampden I
	20 June–16 October 1942	Lancaster I/III

CHAPTER TWENTY-EIGHT

Waddington

Four miles to the south of Lincoln is another of the county's famous RAF airfields. Not only is RAF Waddington known because of its wartime history but also because of its post-war and modern-day eras, when iconic aircraft such as the Vulcan and E-3D have graced the skies over Lincolnshire.

Life for this historic airfield started during the First World War when it opened in 1916 as a flying training station of the Royal Flying Corps. Although having closed in 1919, much of the former airfield remained and from the mid-1920s until the late 1930s it was home to a Special Reserve bombing unit, 503 'County

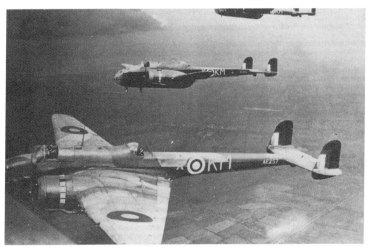

Hampdens of 44 Squadron. At the outbreak of the Second World War, the squadron was based at Waddington and it remained there until May 1943. (Author's collection via Ken Delve)

of Lincoln' Squadron. During those years the squadron flew a number of different types of biplanes from Waddington before the squadron disbanded at the end of 1938. By then, Waddington had been earmarked to be one of Bomber Command's main airfields and so control was passed from 3 Group to 5 Group. Several new bomber squadrons either formed or re-formed at Waddington and soon the airfield was home to three squadrons of Hawker Hinds. But by the outbreak of the Second World War, Waddington was still an all-grass airfield with just two of the squadrons still in residence, 44 and 50 Squadrons, with both having exchanged their Hinds for Hampdens.

Waddington's Hampdens were amongst the first to take part in operations when nine aircraft took part in reconnaissance duties on the opening day of the war. Although the Hampden proved quite manoeuvrable, losses were often high. One unfortunate example was on 12 April 1940 when twelve Hampdens from Waddington were part of a force of more than eighty aircraft tasked with searching for German warships off Norway. It was the largest bombing operation of the war to date but amongst the losses were six Hampdens; accurate anti-aircraft fire and the arrival of German fighters had given the crews little chance.

Another resident Hampden squadron based at Waddington at the outbreak of war was 50 Squadron. Here, members of the squadron are pictured at the airfield in April 1940. (50 Sqn records)

The swift German advance through the Low Countries and France during May and June 1940 saw a number of RAF squadrons withdrawn to the UK. One was 142 Squadron, which arrived at Waddington from France in June 1940 before moving its Battles to Binbrook the following month.

July 1940 saw the departure of 50 Squadron to Lindholme, leaving 44 to operate alone from Waddington. One of the squadron's raids that summer was against Berlin on the night of 25/26 August. The attack by just over a hundred aircraft – a mix of Wellingtons and Hampdens – was in response to devastating raids by German bombers on London and other English cities the previous night. Now seen to be getting their own back, the RAF bombers arrived over Berlin to find the city covered by cloud, making accurate bombing all but impossible, but enough bombs fell within the city to anger Hitler. His subsequent decision to order the Luftwaffe to attack London, rather than to continue its bombing of RAF airfields, proved to be a turning point in the Battle of Britain.

With the entry into service of the new Avro Manchester bomber, 207 Squadron was designated the first unit to take delivery of the new type and so the squadron re-formed at Waddington in November 1940. But the problems of operating a heavier bomber from a grass airfield during the winter months, and the numerous technical problems suffered with the Manchester, meant the squadron's first operations with the Manchester did not take place until the night of 24/25 February 1941 when six aircraft attacked the French Atlantic port of Brest. Although all six aircraft returned to Waddington, one suffered damage having crashed on landing.

Bombs fell on Waddington on 9 May 1941 when German bombers carried out raids against targets in South Yorkshire and the East Midlands. During the course of the night a number of bombs fell on and around the airfield. One of the buildings hit was the NAAFI club, killing seven of the female staff and three airmen, and a nearby air-raid shelter was also destroyed. One of those killed was the manageress of the NAAFI, Constance Raven, and the airmen's club at Waddington today is called the Raven's Club in her memory. Fortunately, though, attacks by enemy raiders were few and far between but these raids did mean that no one could consider themselves safe; no matter where they were.

During the summer of 1941 the Hampdens and Manchesters of the two resident squadrons were joined by a mix of aircraft – Blenheims, Hampdens and Oxfords – belonging to 6 BATF, later re-designated 1506 BATF, a unit that would remain at Waddington for the next eighteen months.

Continuing losses amongst the Manchester crews, as well as engine failures and groundings, had meant the aircraft's operational history was to be cut short and it was not long before the Lancaster was brought into service with 44 Squadron at Waddington being the RAF's first squadron to receive the new type.

As part of Waddington's preparations to receive the Lancaster, 207 Squadron moved out during November. 44 Squadron then handed over its Hampdens to a new Canadian unit being formed at Waddington, 420 Squadron RCAF, and took delivery of its first Lancasters during the winter of 1941/42.

It was a particularly hard winter but changes in squadron personnel and facilities meant the transition to the new type went well. Commanding 44 at this time was Wing Commander Rod Learoyd. Having won the Victoria Cross the year before while serving with 49 Squadron, Learoyd had then commanded 83 Squadron at Scampton earlier in 1941. Learoyd was seemingly known to everyone and his arrival at Waddington in December 1941 to take command of the RAF's first operational Lancaster squadron provided a timely and welcome boost.

The first Lancaster operations took place on the night of 3/4 March 1942 when four aircraft took part in minelaying off the Heligoland approaches. While this might have seemed a routine mission, the squadron was about to take part in a raid that would announce the operational arrival of the Lancaster and become legendary in the history of Bomber Command.

The Lancaster's entry into operational service had provided Bomber Command's new commander-in-chief, Air Marshal Arthur Harris, the opportunity to take his bombing offensive deeper into the heart of Germany. Harris knew the potential of the Lancaster and by April 1942 had two operational squadrons at his disposal, the other being 97 Squadron at Woodhall Spa. Harris now wanted to show the Germans that he could attack anywhere at any time, by day or by night.

Rumours of a special operation had started to spread amongst the crews of the two Lancaster squadrons, particularly as they had been training regularly together at low level. A special training flight involving the two squadrons was carried out on 14 April, which took them down to the south coast of England where the Lancasters joined up for a long transit north to carry out a simulated attack on Inverness before returning to their bases.

Finally, on the morning of 17 April, the training and waiting was over as the crews went to the briefing at their respective bases. While the money was on their target being one of the big German battleships, the crews were somewhat surprised when they found out it was to be the *Maschinenfabrik Augsburg-Nurnberg Aktiengesellschaft* factory at Augsburg, a thousand miles away and deep into southern Germany, believed to be responsible for the production of half of the diesel engines required for Germany's U-boats.

The plan was a particularly daring one as the attack was to be carried out at low level during the last minutes of daylight. Six Lancasters from each squadron, flying in two sections of three, and with the two squadrons flying just a couple of miles apart, were to cross the English Channel from Selsey Bill and coast-in at low level across northern France to the west of Le Havre. They would then continue south at low level before turning east to pass to the south of Paris, from where they would set a heading towards Munich, as if the city was the intended target, before finally turning north to Augsburg. The factory was relatively small and so the attack would require pin-point accuracy from a height below 500 feet if success was to be achieved and so it would take place during the last minutes of daylight so that the bombers could make their escape and return under the cover of darkness.

Because of the large amount of fuel needed to reach the target at low level, each Lancaster was to carry just four 1,000 lb bombs fitted with a delayed fuse of eleven seconds to allow the aircraft to clear the target by the time the bomb detonated. It was to be the first raid of its type and so a number of diversionary raids and fighter sorties over northern France were planned in an attempt to keep the Luftwaffe's fighters away from the attacking force. The weather was forecast to be fine with good visibility and little or no cloud all the way to the target.

It was around 3 pm when the Lancasters got airborne from Waddington. Leading 44 Squadron was 25-year-old Squadron Leader John Nettleton, a South African, flying 'B-Baker'. The two other aircraft in his lead section were flown by Flying Officer Ginger Garwell and Sergeant Dusty Rhodes, while 400 yards behind them was the second section of three led by Flight Lieutenant Nick Sandford, with the two other aircraft flown by Warrant Officers Bert Crum and Joe Beckett.

The diversionary raids had managed to divert enemy fighters but as the Lancasters crossed the French coast at little more than 100 feet, the rear section was spotted by Messerschmitt Bf 109Fs that, by chance, had been returning to their home base. It was a stroke of bad luck for the Lancaster crews.

Beckett was the first to spot the 109s to his left and well above. The Lancasters closed up within the two formations but unfortunately for the rear section, one of the 109 pilots had spotted the bombers at low level. Picking on Crum's aircraft, the lone 109 attacked and within seconds more enemy fighters arrived. Crum, concentrating on nothing other than the survival of his own crew, did not see the demise of Beckett's aircraft as it fell astern the formation and plunged into a field. There were no survivors. It was then the turn of Crum's aircraft to fall to the

Squadron Leader John Nettleton was awarded the Victoria Cross for leading the daring low-level daylight raid against a diesel engine factory at Augsburg on 17 April 1942. Although the raid proved costly for 44 Squadron, it marked the arrival of the Lancaster into the combat arena. (AHB)

109s. With his port engines on fire, Crum instructed the second pilot to safely jettison the bombs before he carried out an almost text-book crash-landing into a field. After detonating the secret equipment inside the aircraft, the crew set fire to the Lancaster and set off into the countryside, owing their lives to the immense skill of Crum. Sandford's aircraft, meanwhile, had also become the focus for the marauding fighters and the stricken Lancaster, last seen with all four engines burning, ploughed into the ground, exploding on impact and killing all on board.

The 109s now turned on the lead section and to the aircraft flown by Dusty Rhodes. With the Lancaster's gun turrets soon jammed, it was impossible for the crew to fight back. The port engines were soon on fire, followed by the starboard, and the Lancaster was last seen to pitch up before plunging vertically into the ground.

Four of Nettleton's formation had gone, in no time at all, and it was now the turn of the two surviving Lancasters, those of Nettleton and Garwell, to fight for their lives. Their aircraft were hit time and time again but just as it looked as if they would follow a similar fate to the others, the 109s hauled off, seemingly out of fuel. Amazingly, the six Lancasters of 97 Squadron, just two miles away, had slipped through unnoticed.

44's two surviving aircraft flew on and reached Augsburg without further incident. The last of the daylight was fading by the time they approached the town from the south, but they had already been spotted and so were greeted by a wall of flak. Inside 'B-Baker', Nettleton's crew remained calm as the Lancaster roared ever closer to the target, despite being hit several times but not enough to deter the crew from releasing their bombs and turning for home.

It was a similar story inside Garwell's 'A-Apple' but the crew had not been quite so lucky. Bombs were released over the factory but the aircraft had been hit repeatedly during the run-in and was now on fire. Finding it impossible to maintain control, Garwell picked an open space and put the Lancaster down as best he could. It then slid across the field and broke in half before finally coming to rest; four of the crew, including Garwell, survived.

Just minutes later, all six of 97's Lancasters were roaring up the valley towards the factory. They had reached Augsburg unscathed but by the time the first section commenced its run-in towards the target, every anti-aircraft gun in the area had put up a barrage of fire. Two of 97's aircraft were shot down during the attack, one from each section, although both crews gallantly pressed on to the factory to release their bombs. The squadron's four surviving Lancasters eventually made it back to Woodhall Spa late that night having been airborne for eight hours (see Woodhall Spa for more about 97 Squadron's part in the raid).

But for Nettleton and his crew it was to be an even longer return and they did not make it back to Waddington. According to the briefing, it should have been getting dark as soon as they were off-target but it would be another hour before the crew considered it to be dark enough to remain unseen. There were then navigational problems and Nettleton eventually landed at Squire's Gate near Blackpool just before 1 am the following day, nearly ten hours after getting airborne. His was the only Lancaster from 44 to have made it back at all.

Of the eighty-five men from the two squadrons who had taken part in the raid, forty-nine were missing, although it would later be discovered that twelve had survived to become prisoners of war. For his outstanding courage and leadership John Nettleton was awarded the Victoria Cross. His citation concludes: *'Squadron Leader Nettleton displayed unflinching determination as well as leadership and valour of the highest order.'*

There was a DFC for each of the officers in Nettleton's crew and DFMs for the rest. When it was known that Ginger Garwell had survived, he was also awarded a DFC and there were awards for the three other survivors of his crew. Plaudits arrived from all over, including a signal from Arthur Harris, which included:

The following message has been received from the Prime Minister – 'We must plainly regard the attack of the Lancasters on the U-boat engine factory at Augsburg as an outstanding achievement of the Royal Air Force. Undeterred by heavy losses at the outset, 44 and 97 Squadrons pierced and struck a vital point with deadly precision in broad daylight. Pray convey the thanks of His Majesty's Government to the officers and men who accomplished this memorial feat of arms in which no life was lost in vain.'

There was also a message from Sir Charles Portal, the Chief of the Air Staff:

I would like 44 and 97 Squadrons to know the great importance I attach to this gallant and successful attack on the diesel engine factory at Augsburg. Please give my warmest congratulations and thanks.

Meanwhile, Harris summed up his own thoughts:

The resounding blow which has been struck at the enemy's submarine and tank building programme will echo round the world. The full effects on his submarine campaign cannot be immediately apparent but nevertheless they will be enormous. The gallant adventure penetrating deep into the heart of Germany in daylight and pressed with outstanding determination in the face of bitter and foreseen opposition takes its place amongst the most courageous operations of the war. It is, moreover, yet another fine example of effective co-operation with the other Services by striking at the very sources of enemy effort. The officers and men who took part, those who returned and those who fell, have indeed deserved well of their country.

After the raid, John Nettleton was sent on a tour of the United States to promote the Allied war effort. He then returned to Waddington in June to take command of the newly formed 1661 HCU before he was given command of 44 Squadron six months later.

While 44 Squadron had been involved in the Augsburg raid, 420 Squadron RCAF had continued to operate its Hampdens from Waddington before, in August 1942, the squadron was transferred to 4 Group and moved out. During the same month, 9 Squadron moved to Waddington to replace its Wellingtons with Lancasters.

By March 1943 Waddington was in desperate need of an upgrade, specifically to have hardened runways, and so 9 and 44 Squadrons moved out. Eight months later, with work complete, the airfield re-opened with the first unit to arrive being the Australians of 467 (RAAF) Squadron, and, just days later, 463

The legendary R5868 in the 'PO-S Sugar' markings of 467 (RAAF) Squadron at Waddington. The aircraft flew the last seventy or so of its operational sorties, believed to have totalled 136, with the squadron, the vast majority of which were flown from Waddington. The aircraft is now in the RAF Museum at Hendon and is credited as being the oldest and highest operational (number of ops) surviving Lancaster. (AHB)

(RAAF) Squadron formed at Waddington from a nucleus of 467 personnel.

Waddington had now been designated Headquarters 53 Base as part of Bomber Command's re-organization with the administrative and technical control of the nearby airfields of Bardney and Skellingthorpe. It was the start of the Battle of Berlin and like all Bomber Command squadrons, the Aussies fought hard and had to suffer losses along the way. It was a particularly hard and costly introduction to operations for 463, with the squadron suffering the highest losses of the county's Australian bomber squadrons.

Both Australian squadrons remained at Waddington until the end of the war. With hostilities over, they moved out and over the next couple of years several Bomber Command squadrons were based at Waddington at one time or another. The Lancasters were phased out of service and replaced by the Avro Lincoln, but by 1953 all the Lincolns had left as plans had already been made to prepare Waddington for the arrival of the new V-bombers that were about to enter service with the RAF.

As part of the preparations the three concrete runways were replaced by one lengthened runway of 9,000 feet, which meant the A15 had to be re-routed so that the runway could be sufficiently extended. Work was completed in 1955 but the first aircraft to operate from the new airfield were not V-bombers but Canberras. However, by the beginning of 1957 the first Vulcans were ready for delivery to Waddington and so the Canberras moved out.

Waddington's long association with the Vulcan during the Cold War lasted well into the 1980s. The station also became involved in the Falklands conflict of 1982 when, under Operation *Black Buck*, Vulcans deployed to Ascension Island and took part in long-range bombing missions of Argentine positions in and around the capital of Port Stanley. Then, after the conflict was over, a shortage of RAF refuelling aircraft in the UK led to Waddington's Vulcans being modified as single-point air-to-air refuelling aircraft. Finally, the end of the Vulcan era came in 1984 when the last squadron disbanded at Waddington.

RAF Waddington today, viewed from the main A15 into Lincoln with Vulcan XM607, which flew the first bombing raid against the airfield at Port Stanley during the Falklands conflict of 1982, standing proudly as the station's guardian. (Author)

Waddington was maintained as a major RAF base and hosted a number of NATO aircraft, either on exercise or when visiting the North Sea Air Combat Range, which was facilitated from Waddington. Then, in 1991, the airfield became home to the new Boeing E-3D Airborne Early Warning (AEW) aircraft entering service with the RAF and four years later Nimrod R1s arrived from Wyton to operate in the reconnaissance role. Today Waddington is the RAF's hub for intelligence, surveillance, target acquisition and reconnaissance (ISTAR) to support national and NATO operations using a range of aircraft and platforms, including the airfield's long-standing resident, the E-3D Sentry.

Understandably, there are several reminders of Waddington's wartime history, including the Nettleton Room, and the post-war reminders include Vulcan XM607, which stands proudly alongside the A15. There is also the Waddington Heritage Centre but access to the station is by prior permission only.

Summary of Waddington during the Second World War

Squadron	Date	Aircraft type
44 Squadron	June 1937–30 May 1943	Hampden/Lancaster
50 Squadron	May 1937–9 July 1940	Hampden
142 Squadron	15 June–2 July 1940	Battle I
207 Squadron	1 November 1940–16 November 1941	Manchester I
420 Squadron RCAF	19 December 1941–5 August 1942	Hampden/ Manchester
9 Squadron	7 August 1942–13 April 1943	Lancaster I/III
467 (RAAF) Squadron	12 November 1943–15 June 1945	Lancaster I/III
463 (RAAF) Squadron	25 November 1943–2 July 1945	Lancaster I/III

CHAPTER TWENTY-NINE

Woodhall Spa

Another wartime airfield built as part of Bomber Command's expansion scheme was Woodhall Spa. The site was first identified by the Air Ministry as suitable for development as a satellite for Coningsby. Work began in early 1941 and just a year later the airfield was considered ready. The airfield opened in February 1942 but as one of 5 Group's smaller airfields it could only accommodate one squadron.

The first unit to arrive at Woodhall Spa was 97 Squadron, equipped with Lancasters, which moved in from nearby Coningsby in March. The squadron was Bomber Command's second to become operational with the new Lancaster (the first being 44 Squadron at Waddington) and was soon in action from the new airfield in what was to become one of the legendary bomber raids of the Second World War.

On 17 April the two new Lancaster squadrons took part in the daring low level daylight raid against a diesel engine factory at Augsburg (see Waddington for more about the raid). The raid involved six Lancasters from both 44 and 97 Squadrons, with those of 97 led by 23-year-old Squadron Leader John Sherwood, an experienced pilot with a DFC and Bar.

Flying in two sections of three, the 97 Lancasters set off from Woodhall Spa in mid-afternoon for the long transit to the target. Because of the amount of fuel required for the raid, each aircraft was carrying just four 1,000 lb bombs fitted with a delayed fuse of eleven seconds to allow the aircraft to clear the target by the time the bomb detonated.

As the Lancasters crossed the northern coastline of France at little more than 100 feet, the two sections of 44 Squadron were spotted by Messerschmitt Bf 109s. It was a stroke of bad luck and in a matter of just a few minutes, four of 44's six Lancasters were shot down. Quite remarkably, though, the six aircraft of 97 Squadron, just two miles away from the carnage, managed to slip through unnoticed and reached Augsburg without incident.

By the time Sherwood's formation approached the town from the south it was nearly 8 pm. The two surviving aircraft from 44 had already attacked and so the defences were now fully alert. As the six aircraft roared up the valley towards the factory every anti-aircraft gun put up a barrage of fire.

In the lead aircraft, Sherwood did not flinch. He was charging as fast and as low as he dare through what had now become a horrendous wall of fire. He could have asked no more of his two wingmen, Flying Officers Darky Hallows and Rod Rodley. Both were relatively inexperienced in terms of operations, with just six and eight ops respectively, but they continued to stick to their leader like glue, just as they had done since leaving Woodhall Spa five hours before.

To anyone observing the scene, it would have seemed all but impossible for anything to get through the defensive barrage that now filled the sky, but the three Lancasters just kept pressing on towards their target. Sherwood then eased up over the chimneys before dropping back down to finally release his bombs.

Just seconds behind, Hallows and Rodley made their final adjustments before completing their attacks. It was at that point that Rodley saw Sherwood's aircraft emitting smoke as it turned starboard to escape to the north at which point it burst into flames. As the bombs from 97's lead section exploded on their target, Sherwood's Lancaster smashed into the ground.

With Hallows and Rodley starting their long journey home, the rear section of 97 were on the final part of their run-in towards the factory. Being the last to attack, the pilots had been carefully selected and were amongst some of the most experienced within Bomber Command. Flight Lieutenant David Penman, leading the section, was on his second operational tour and a holder of the DFC while Flying Officer Ernest Deverill DFM had flown more than a hundred operational sorties, mainly with Coastal Command, and Warrant Officer Tommy Mycock was another holder of the DFC.

The three Lancasters came under intense anti-aircraft fire. The German gunners had long established the exact line of attack but Penman held his aircraft as steady as possible, despite being hit several times. The Lancasters were now just three miles from the target but Mycock's Lancaster suddenly received a devastating burst of fire, causing an immediate fire that quickly spread through the aircraft. It was a mortal blow but Mycroft used all of his experience to hold the Lancaster steady for long enough to reach the target and for the bombs to be released. His aircraft was then seen to pull up and swing to the left before plunging into the ground.

Penman and Deverill, meanwhile, had succeeded in getting through the wall of flak and had completed their attacks. It was a long transit home but the four surviving aircraft from the two sections made it safely back to Woodhall Spa, landing at around 11 pm having been airborne for eight hours.

For his outstanding leadership of the raid, John Nettleton of 44 Squadron was awarded the Victoria Cross. Also recommended for the VC was John Sherwood who had so gallantly led the 97 Squadron formation. As with Nettleton's award, the recommendation was endorsed by Harris but someone in the Air Ministry scrawled '*to be recommended for DSO if later found to be alive*'.

Miraculously, Sherwood was later found to be alive, although the rest of his crew had been killed, and so he received the DSO. But it has long been suggested that John Sherwood should also have received the Victoria Cross; would two awards of the VC for the same raid really have been too much? It had happened before.

In addition to Sherwood's DSO there were a number of other awards for 97's survivors of the raid. There was a DSO for David Penman for his great skill in the handling of the rear section and for the greatest determination in attacking the target from very low level in spite of intense and accurate anti-aircraft fire. There was a DFC for Darky Hallows, for taking over the lead section after Sherwood had been shot down, and for displaying great courage and determination throughout the raid. The two other surviving captains, Rod Rodley and Ernest Deverill, both received the DFC, as did Penman's second pilot and his observer, and there were six DFMs awarded to other squadron survivors of the raid. Although many felt Tommy Mycock's courage should have been recognized with a VC, he was instead awarded a posthumous Mentioned in Despatches, as were others killed in the raid.

The Lancasters had caused sufficient damage to hold up diesel engine production at the factory for several weeks. News of the raid soon spread and plaudits arrived from the highest levels (see Waddington for more about the aftermath of the Augsburg raid).

97 Squadron remained at Woodhall Spa for a further year before moving in April 1943 to become part of the Pathfinder Force. Replacing 97 was a new Lancaster squadron, 619 Squadron, which formed at Woodhall the same month. The squadron flew its first operation on the night of 11/12 June during what was the height of Bomber Command's offensive against German industrial targets in the Ruhr. On this particular night the target was Düsseldorf with 619 contributing twelve Lancasters to a raiding force of nearly 800 aircraft; one of 619's aircraft failed to return.

Like all bomber airfields, Woodhall suffered losses and the worst night of the summer of 1943 was on the night of 17/18 August. It was one of Bomber Command's special raids and the target was the German V-weapon research establishment at Peenemünde on the Baltic coast. For the first time a Master Bomber was allocated to the raid and the attack was carried out in moonlit conditions to give the bombers every chance of identifying what was a small target. The plan worked and it was later estimated that the raid caused a setback in the German V-weapons programme, but forty aircraft were lost during the raid, including three of 619's Lancasters and amongst those killed was the squadron commander, Wing Commander Irwin McGhie.

McGhie was replaced by Wing Commander 'Jock' Abercrombie who led the squadron for the rest of the year. Life for the aircrew at Woodhall was generally very good. When not on duty the officers were able to enjoy their magnificent surroundings of the Petwood Hotel. The hotel was built at the turn of the century as a house for Lady Weighall on a site chosen by her in the area of her favourite 'pet wood'. It had been requisitioned by the Air Ministry in 1943 and became the Officers' Mess for 617 Squadron with the station commander at the time, Group Captain Peter Johnson, accommodated in the bridal suite.

Leonard Cheshire commanded 617 Squadron at Woodhall Spa during 1944 and was awarded the Victoria Cross having completed his fourth tour of operations, totalling 100 operational sorties. It was the only occasion when a VC was awarded for a prolonged period of operations rather than for a specific act. (AHB)

619 moved to Coningsby at the beginning of 1944, exchanging places with 617 Squadron, the legendary Dambusters, now under the command of Wing Commander Leonard Cheshire. Because Woodhall could only accommodate one squadron it was considered ideal for 617. Since carrying out the Dams raid in May 1943, 617 had moved to Coningsby where it had been working up in its role as a specialist bombing squadron before its move to Woodhall in January 1944.

On the night of 8/9 February, the squadron sent twelve aircraft to attack the Gnome-Rhône aero-engine factory at Limoges. It was an important raid for many reasons. Cheshire wanted to prove his theory of marking a target at low-level. Until that point, high-level marking and specialist bombing, particularly against targets in France, had been unsatisfactory with the loss of many French lives. In this case, the factory at Limoges was surrounded by French houses and so it was important to achieve precision during the attack.

The aircraft arrived over the target to find the factory undefended and quite visible in the bright moonlight. Cheshire

Located in magnificent grounds of woodland and extended gardens, the Petwood Hotel was home to the officers based at Woodhall Spa during the Second World War. Inside the hotel there remain many reminders of the Lancaster crews who flew from the airfield and the hotel's squadron bar is dedicated to the men of 617 Squadron. (Author)

first carried out three runs over the factory before he was satisfied that the French workers had been given enough warning that an attack was about to take place. Then, on his fourth run, at less than 100 feet, he dropped his 30 lb incendiaries. The eleven Lancasters then released their 12,000 lb bombs with devastating accuracy; ten bombs hit the target while the eleventh fell into a river nearby. There were few, if any, French casualties and all the aircraft returned safely to base.

The raid had been a success and carried out with text book accuracy. It had identified a new method to accurately mark targets at night. But flying a Lancaster below 100 feet at night, particularly over built-up areas, was not easy and so Cheshire would soon be granted his request for the squadron to receive a handful of smaller and highly manoeuvrable Mosquitos.

But it was not all to be success. Four nights later, ten Lancasters attempted to bomb the Anthéor viaduct, an important rail link between France and Italy. Two aircraft carried out low-level runs to mark the target. One was flown by Cheshire and the other by Squadron Leader Micky Martin, a long-term member of the squadron and survivor of the Dams raid, but the viaduct was heavily defended and the sides of the valley very steep. Both aircraft were hit, killing Martin's bomb aimer, Flight Lieutenant Bob Hay, the squadron's bombing leader, who had flown on the Dams raid with Martin.

One pilot to have joined 617 earlier in the year was Flight Lieutenant Bill Reid VC who had now recovered from wounds received during the raid against Dusseldorf on the night that had earned him the Victoria Cross. Reid had taken with him his bomb aimer from his 61 Squadron crew, Flight Sergeant Les Rolton, whom he had been with since their early days of training. The two men joined up with their new crew and then went through weeks of specialist training before they were ready to take part in their first operation with 617 on the night of 18/19 April 1944; it was a raid against the railway marshalling yards at Juvisy on the outskirts of Paris.

It was also during April 1944 that Pathfinder Mosquito IVs of 627 Squadron arrived at Woodhall Spa. The Mosquitos had initially formed part of the Light Night Striking Force to supplement Bomber Command's major raids but had now been transferred to 5 Group to work alongside the Lancasters of 617.

Cheshire had also secured his own Mosquitos and used four to provide target-marking for a main force attack against Munich on the night of 24/25 April. It was to be something of an experiment for the squadron as it would further test Cheshire's new method of target-marking at low level against a heavily defended target deep in enemy territory. The Mosquitos would be on the limit of their range, with very little fuel to spare, and so marking would have to be carried out quickly and accurately. In addition to Cheshire's section of four, eleven Mossies of 627 Squadron were also to take part in the raid, their task being to fly ahead of the main bombing force to drop 'Window' (strips of aluminium foil) over the target to disrupt the German's radar system.

Cheshire flew one of the Mosquitos with the three others flown by Dave Shannon, another survivor of the Dams raid, Gerry Fawkes and Terry Kearns. The four aircraft first flew to Manston to refuel before flying directly to the target. It was the early hours of the following morning when they arrived over the target. Cheshire was immediately 'coned' by searchlights and dived down to low level to run-in and mark the target. Despite the fact that all guns within range opened up against him, Cheshire flew in at 700 feet to drop his markers with great accuracy.

The other Mosquitos had done their bit too, dropping their markers with the same precision. While the main force carried out the attack, Cheshire remained overhead the city at 1,000 feet to assess the accuracy of the marking and to direct the bombing of other aircraft during the attack, despite his own aircraft having been hit several times. Finally satisfied the attack had been a success, he turned for home and landed safely back at Manston with hardly a drop of fuel left. Post-raid reconnaissance the following morning showed the attack on Munich had been a success, with considerable damage done to the railway installations and many buildings destroyed.

The Mosquitos of 627 Squadron were used to provide low-level marking for the first time against Schweinfurt on the night of 26/27 April but the raid was not a success. A strong headwind had delayed the main force of bombers and German night fighters had capitalized on the fact that the 200-plus Lancasters had become stretched. Consequently, the bombing was not accurate, with most of the bombs falling outside the city and twenty-one Lancasters were lost – nearly 10 per cent of the attacking force.

617's Lancasters were now modified to carry the new 12,000 lb high-explosive and deep-penetration bomb called Tallboy (see *Bomber Command in the Second World War* for a description of the Tallboy). The first Tallboy attack was carried out on the night of 8/9 June 1944, just two days after the D-Day landings. The target was a railway tunnel near Saumur, just over a hundred miles to the south of the main battle area of Normandy. Intelligence had been received that a German Panzer division was expected to move forward and pass through the tunnel towards the Allied beachhead. The railway was the main south-to-north route on the Loire and with the Allies having only landed in France just forty-eight hours before, their position was still precarious and so the tunnel had to be destroyed.

Led by Cheshire, twenty-five Lancasters took off for the raid; nineteen were armed with Tallboys while the other six were more conventionally armed. The target area was illuminated with flares by four Pathfinder Lancasters from nearby Coningsby and marked at low level by three of 617's Mosquitos. 617's Lancasters then dropped their Tallboys and conventional bombs with great accuracy. One pierced the roof of the tunnel while the others fell all around, the shock causing massive destruction and resulting in large rocks and huge amounts of soil blocking the tunnel for some considerable time and so delaying the arrival of the Panzers.

The first Tallboy raid had been a huge success and without loss. Then, the following week, on 14 June, the squadron carried out a further Tallboy raid, this time against the French port of Le Havre. It was part of a much bigger effort against the port with 617 opening proceedings with twenty-two Tallboy-equipped aircraft, again led by Cheshire, attacking the concrete German E-boat pens just before the first of two waves of main force bombers attacked the port in the last hours of daylight. It had been Bomber Command's first daylight raid for more than a year and the threat of German E-boats to the landing beachhead had all but been removed.

By now Hitler had launched the first of his terror weapons against southern England, and so 617 Squadron was given the task of attacking the V-weapon sites in the Pas de Calais as part of Operation *Crossbow*. After standing by for three days waiting for cloud over northern France to clear, the first use of Tallboy against the V-sites took place on 19 June. The target was a large concrete flying bomb storage facility at Watten near St Omer. Nineteen of the squadron's Lancasters and two Mosquitos took part in the raid. Weather conditions were not good and so it made any assessment of the raid all but impossible, but one Tallboy is believed to have landed around fifty yards from the target, making the storage bunker useless.

Five days later, on 24 June, sixteen of 617's Lancasters bombed the Wizernes site, their Tallboys causing more devastation. One Lancaster was shot down, the squadron's first loss for two months. The following day, the squadron sent seventeen aircraft to bomb the V-weapon storage facility at Siracourt. This time Cheshire carried out the target-marking at low level in a Mustang fighter, courtesy of the American Air Force, which had only arrived at Woodhall Spa that afternoon. It was his first flight in the type and so his first landing was in the dark. Three of the Tallboys scored direct hits against the concrete facility and no aircraft were lost.

It had been an intense period of operations but attacks against the V-sites were far from over, although the next Tallboy attack did not take place until 4 July when seventeen Lancasters carried out a daylight attack against the large V-1 flying bomb storage facility at St-Leu-d'Esserent, located in a large cave to the north of Paris. The raid was followed up by a further attack on the site that night by Bomber Command's Main Force. Then, on 6 July, the squadron's Tallboy-equipped Lancasters carried out an attack on another V-site, this time at Mimoyecques.

Cheshire had now flown his 100th operational sortie and was withdrawn from operations. He had far exceeded what could have reasonably been expected of him and soon after came the announcement that he was to be awarded the Victoria Cross. It was the only time a VC was awarded to an airman for an extensive period of operations rather than for a specific act. Also ordered to rest from operations were 617's three flight commanders – Squadron Leaders Joe McCarthy, Les Munro and Dave Shannon; all were survivors of the Dams raid more than a year before.

Replacing Cheshire was Wing Commander James 'Willie' Tait, a highly decorated and extremely experienced bomber pilot with a DSO and two Bars and a DFC. The raids against the V-weapons facilities went on, with three more Tallboy attacks carried out that month. The first was another attack against Wizernes on 17 July, followed by another raid against Watten on 27 July, before the third Tallboy attack was planned for 31 July, this time against a V-weapon storage site located in a railway tunnel at Rilly-la-Montagne, near Rheims.

For this latest raid the squadron's Lancasters joined forces with others of Bomber Command and it was a raid where the luck of one of 617's pilots finally ran out. Having released his Tallboy from 12,000 feet right on cue, Bill Reid's Lancaster was then rocked as a 1,000 lb bomb dropped from a Lancaster above passed straight through his aircraft mid-way along the fuselage. Although there was no explosion, the bomb had severed the control cables of Reid's aircraft. Unable to maintain control, Reid gave the order to his crew to bale out but as the crew tried to make their escape the aircraft went into a dive, pinning Reid to his seat. Struggling with the forces, Reid finally managed to release the escape hatch and get out, just seconds before the Lancaster broke in two. Reid was captured and taken as a prisoner of war but two gunners had died in the rear section of the fuselage while three met their deaths in the forward section, including Reid's long-term crew colleague and friend, Les Rolton.

During September 1944, 617 Squadron joined forces with 9 Squadron at Bardney to carry out Operation *Paravane*, an attack against the mighty German battleship *Tirpitz*, at the time anchored in the Kåfjord in northern Norway. When carrying a Tallboy, the Lancaster did not have the range to reach the fjord from a British base and so the Russians agreed to allow the Lancasters to use one of their airfields at Yagodnik near Archangel, around 600 miles from where *Tirpitz* was anchored.

The attack against *Tirpitz* was to be carried out by twenty aircraft of 617, led by Willie Tait, and eighteen from 9 Squadron (see Bardney for further details of the raid). After setting off from their bases in Lincolnshire on 11 September, the Lancasters first landed at Lossiemouth in Scotland to refuel before setting off for the long journey to Russia, while two B-24 Liberators carried the ground crew and a Mosquito headed for Yagodnik to carry out a reconnaissance mission ahead of the raid.

But bad weather encountered over Russia meant the Lancasters became scattered and crews were left to land wherever they could; six aircraft crash-landed in marshes. Even some of those that had managed to land safely required repairs and would not be fit to take part in the raid.

By the morning of the 14th all surviving aircraft had gathered at Yagodnik. The weather was favourable for the following day and after the Mosquito returned from its early morning reconnaissance sortie, confirming that *Tirpitz* was still at anchor and that the weather was suitable over the fjord, the decision was made to carry out the attack.

Around 6.30 am on 15 September, twenty-eight Lancasters took off to attack *Tirpitz*. Twenty were carrying Tallboys and seven carried 500 lb Johnny Walker mines, specifically designed for attacking ships in shallow water, while the remaining aircraft was to film the raid.

As would be expected, *Tirpitz* was well protected in the narrow fjord by a complex defence system of a smoke screen and anti-aircraft flak batteries. But the Lancasters clearly caught the defences by surprise. There were no fighters to be seen and the flak was ineffective. However, *Tirpitz* soon became hidden by the smoke, making bombing difficult. Even so, seventeen Tallboys were dropped, as were all the Johnny Walker mines.

The post-raid reconnaissance by the Mosquito just two hours later had not been able to assess the result of the raid because of the build-up of cloud. All that could be determined was that *Tirpitz* was still afloat. The Lancasters returned to the UK, although one of 617's aircraft, flown by Flying Officer Frank Levy, was lost over Norway on its way home.

Any thoughts of returning to complete the job against *Tirpitz* had to be put to one side as once back at Woodhall the crews were straight back into their more routine duties. It was also during September that Bomber Command suffered a tragic loss when Wing Commander Guy Gibson was killed while flying from the airfield. At the time Gibson was on a non-operational staff tour at nearby Coningsby but he had managed to grab the occasional operational sortie whenever the opportunity presented itself. On the evening of 19 September Gibson took off from Woodhall Spa in a Mosquito belonging to 627 Squadron to act as Master Bomber for a raid against Rheydt and Mönchengladbach. Flying with him was Coningsby's station navigation officer, Squadron Leader James Warwick. Gibson was last heard over the target area late that evening, after which his aircraft was seen to come down in flames at Steenbergen in Holland where it exploded on impact.

At first it was not known that Gibson's aircraft was overdue. With Woodhall Spa and Coningsby being so close together, each airfield assumed the Mosquito had landed at the other. And when that turned out not to be the case, the hope was that the aircraft had landed elsewhere. But it soon became apparent that the aircraft was lost. At the time of his death, Guy Gibson was just twenty-six. Of all the RAF's VC winners, few, if any, will be better known than Wing Commander Guy Gibson VC DSO and Bar DFC and Bar.

Word of Gibson's loss soon spread but there was no time to dwell. On the night of 23/24 September, 617 Squadron returned to attack the Dortmund-Ems Canal, a target that had cost the squadron heavy losses a year before. Carrying Tallboys, the squadron's task was to bomb the banks of the two parallel branches of the canal at a point near Ladbergen, north of Münster, where the level of the water was well above the surrounding countryside. Two direct hits caused breaches in the banks of both branches of the canal, resulting in a six-mile stretch being drained.

Meanwhile, despite its apparent lack of seaworthiness, *Tirpitz* had remained a high priority. She was now known to have moved further south near Tromsø for use as a heavy artillery battery, and so it meant that a raid could at last be mounted from Scotland. Lancasters of 617 and 9 Squadrons again flew north to Lossiemouth and, on 29 October, Tait led another attack against *Tirpitz*. Thirty-seven aircraft took part in the raid, eighteen from each squadron plus the film unit, but the attack was unsuccessful. Heavy cloud had formed shortly before the bombers arrived, making it all but impossible to see *Tirpitz*. Thirty-two aircraft bombed but no Tallboys hit. One of 617's aircraft was damaged by flak but managed to crash-land in Sweden.

Once again, *Tirpitz* had survived but then, on 12 November, Tait led a third attack with a force of thirty Lancasters from the same two squadrons plus the film unit. This time the weather was clear and *Tirpitz* was hit by at least two Tallboys, causing the mighty battleship to capsize once and for all. Several messages of congratulations arrived at both squadrons from the highest levels, including a message from the King who said 'please convey my hearty congratulations to all those who took part in the daring and successful attack on the *Tirpitz*' and from the Prime Minister, Winston Churchill, who offered his 'heartiest congratulations to all'.

Tait was rested from operations the following month. Like Cheshire, he had completed a hundred operations and was now awarded a third Bar to his DSO for his conspicuous bravery and extreme devotion to duty in the face of the enemy; he was one of only two in the RAF to have been awarded the DSO four times.

617 Squadron continued its specialist bombing role from Woodhall Spa until the end of the war. On 14 March 1945, a specially modified Lancaster flown by Squadron Leader 'Jock' Calder dropped the first of another new bomb, the 22,000 lb

Grand Slam, on the Schildesche viaduct at Bielefeld (see Bomber Command in the Second World War for more about the Grand Slam). The bomb was dropped from 12,000 feet and shattered the target, causing the viaduct to collapse.

By the end of the war forty-two Grand Slams had been dropped. Then, with hostilities over, 617 Squadron moved to Waddington to leave the Mosquitos of 627 Squadron as Woodhall's only residents.

Although the war was over, the dangers of operating aircraft from the airfield remained and one example of the extreme courage displayed by RAF ground crew, both during and after hostilities, is that of Corporal Stephen Cogger who was in charge of the fire section at Woodhall Spa on the afternoon of 3 July. Cogger was awarded the GM for his bravery following a crash-landing of a Mosquito after the aircraft overshot the runway into a field and caught fire. Cogger was first on the scene and made a number of forays into the flames to rescue the trapped navigator. In spite of his own burns, Cogger managed to cut the navigator free and he then went back into the fire to try and rescue the pilot. But the pilot could not be reached and was already dead. Cogger was then rushed to hospital suffering from major burns

On the B1192 between Woodhall Spa and Coningsby is the Thorpe Camp Visitors' Centre, situated on what was the communal site of the airfield and dedicated to Woodhall Spa and its squadrons during the Second World War. (Author)

In the centre of the village of Woodhall Spa is the 617 Squadron Dambusters memorial and a more recent memorial (far right) in memory of all members of the squadron who have given their lives since 1945 in service of their country. (Author)

to his face, arms and hands. He had displayed great gallantry in circumstances when, at any moment, the aircraft might have exploded.

By October 1945 the Mosquitos had moved out and the airfield closed to flying, although the land was retained by the Air Ministry. During the mid-1960s Woodhall Spa was home to Bloodhound surface-to-air missiles and after the missiles had gone the north-western part of the airfield and a hangar was retained until 2003 as an engine-testing facility for nearby Coningsby.

Little of this former airfield can be seen but the area can be reached by taking the B1192 from Woodhall Spa towards Coningsby. The road runs along the western boundary of the old airfield and further along is the Thorpe Camp Visitors' Centre, situated on what was once the communal site, which, amongst other things, remembers RAF Woodhall Spa and its squadrons during the Second World War.

In the centre of the village of Woodhall Spa, in the Royal Square Gardens at the junction of the B1191 and B1192, stands the impressive Dambusters Memorial as a tribute to those members of 617 Squadron who failed to return from operations during the war. Also in the gardens is a new memorial in memory of those members of the squadron who have given their lives since 1945 in service of their country. In the village church (St Peter) is a memorial plaque to 619 Squadron, dedicated to all those who served with the squadron between 1943 and 1945, while inside the Petwood Hotel, the Officers' Mess between 1943 and 1945, many reminders of the wartime days can be found. These include the squadron bar, dedicated to the men of 617 Squadron, and the RAF ensign regularly flies proudly from the hotel.

Summary of Woodhall Spa during the Second World War

Squadron	Date	Aircraft type
97 Squadron	2 March 1942–17 April 1943	Lancaster I/III
619 Squadron	18 April 1943–8 January 1944	Lancaster I/III
617 Squadron	10 January 1944–16 June 1945	Lancaster I/III
627 Squadron	15 April 1944–30 September 1945	Mosquito IV/XVI/XX/XXV

Appendix 1

Lincolnshire's Victoria Crosses of Bomber Command

Recipient	Sqn	Airfield	Date of Act (Target)
F/L Rod Learoyd	49 Sqn	Scampton	12/13 Aug 40 (Dortmund-Ems Canal)
Sgt John Hannah	83 Sqn	Scampton	15/16 Sep 40 (Invasion barges Antwerp)
S/L John Nettleton	44 Sqn	Waddington	17 Apr 42 (Augsburg)
F/O Leslie Manser	50 Sqn	Skellingthorpe	30/31 May 42 (Cologne)
W/C Guy Gibson	617 Sqn	Scampton	16/17 May 43 (Ruhr Dams)
Sgt Norman Jackson	106 Sqn	Metheringham	26/27 Apr 44 (Schweinfurt)
W/C Leonard Cheshire	617 Sqn	Woodhall Spa	(Sustained period of 100 ops 1940–44)
F/S George Thompson	9 Sqn	Bardney	1 Jan 45 (Dortmund-Ems Canal)

APPENDIX 2

Group Commanders 1939–45

(1 Group and 5 Group only)

1 Group

Air Vice-Marshal A C Wright	3 September–22 December 1939 (1 Group became Advanced Air Striking Force and then temporarily disbanded)
Air Commodore J J Breen	27 June–27 November 1940
Air Vice-Marshal R D Oxland	27 November 1940–24 February 1943
Air Vice-Marshal E A B Rice	24 February 1943–12 February 1945
Air Vice-Marshal R S Blucke	12 February 1945–

5 Group

Air Commodore W B Calloway	17 August 1937–11 September 1939
Air Vice-Marshal A T Harris	11 September 1939–22 November 1940
Air Vice-Marshal N H Bottomley	22 November 1940–12 May 1941
Air Vice-Marshal J C Slessor	12 May 1941–25 April 1942
Air Vice-Marshal W A Coryton	25 April 1942–28 February 1943
Air Vice-Marshal The Hon R A Cochrane	28 February 1943–16 January 1945
Air Vice-Marshal H A Constantine	16 January 1945–

APPENDIX 3

Order of Battle 1939–40

(Operational Squadrons Based in Lincolnshire Only)

31 August 1939

5 Group

44 Sqn	Waddington	Hampden
49 Sqn	Scampton	Hampden
50 Sqn	Waddington	Hampden
61 Sqn	Hemswell	Hampden
83 Sqn	Scampton	Hampden
144 Sqn	Hemswell	Hampden

14 November 1940

1 Group

12 Sqn	Binbrook	Wellington
142 Sqn	Binbrook	Wellington
300 (Polish) Sqn	Swinderby	Wellington
301 (Polish) Sqn	Swinderby	Wellington

5 Group

44 Sqn	Waddington	Hampden
49 Sqn	Scampton	Hampden
61 Sqn	Hemswell	Hampden
83 Sqn	Scampton	Hampden
144 Sqn	Hemswell	Hampden
207 Sqn	Waddington	Manchester

APPENDIX 4

Order of Battle – February 1942

(Operational Squadrons Based in Lincolnshire Only)

1 Group

12 Sqn	Binbrook	Wellington
103 Sqn	Elsham Wolds	Wellington
142 Sqn	Grimsby	Wellington
300 (Polish) Sqn	Hemswell	Wellington
301 (Polish) Sqn	Hemswell	Wellington

5 Group

44 Sqn	Waddington	Lancaster
49 Sqn	Scampton	Hampden
50 Sqn	Skellingthorpe	Hampden
83 Sqn	Scampton	Manchester
97 Sqn	Coningsby	Lancaster
106 Sqn	Coningsby	Hampden
420 Sqn RCAF	Waddington	Hampden

Appendix 5

Order of Battle – February 1943

(Operational Squadrons Based in Lincolnshire Only)

1 Group

12 Sqn	Wickenby	Lancaster
100 Sqn	Grimsby	Lancaster
103 Sqn	Elsham Wolds	Lancaster
166 Sqn	Kirmington	Wellington
199 Sqn	Ingham	Wellington
300 (Polish) Sqn	Hemswell	Wellington
301 (Polish) Sqn	Hemswell	Wellington
305 (Polish) Sqn	Hemswell	Wellington

5 Group

9 Sqn	Waddington	Lancaster
44 Sqn	Waddington	Lancaster
49 Sqn	Fiskerton	Lancaster
50 Sqn	Skellingthorpe	Lancaster
57 Sqn	Scampton	Lancaster
97 Sqn	Woodhall Spa	Lancaster

APPENDIX 6

Order of Battle – November 1943 (Battle of Berlin)

(Operational Squadrons Based in Lincolnshire Only)

1 Group

12 Sqn	Wickenby	Lancaster
100 Sqn	Grimsby	Lancaster
101 Sqn	Ludford Magna	Lancaster
103 Sqn	Elsham Wolds	Lancaster
166 Sqn	Kirmington	Lancaster
460 (RAAF) Sqn	Binbrook	Lancaster
550 Sqn	Grimsby	Lancaster
576 Sqn	Elsham Wolds	Lancaster
625 Sqn	Kelstern	Lancaster
626 Sqn	Wickenby	Lancaster

5 Group

9 Sqn	Bardney	Lancaster
44 Sqn	Dunholme Lodge	Lancaster
49 Sqn	Fiskerton	Lancaster
50 Sqn	Skellingthorpe	Lancaster
57 Sqn	East Kirkby	Lancaster
61 Sqn	Skellingthorpe	Lancaster
463 (RAAF) Sqn	Waddington	Lancaster
467 (RAAF) Sqn	Waddington	Lancaster
619 Sqn	Woodhall Spa	Lancaster
630 Sqn	East Kirkby	Lancaster

APPENDIX 7

Order of Battle – January 1945

(Operational Squadrons Based in Lincolnshire Only)

1 Group

12 Sqn	Wickenby	Lancaster
100 Sqn	Grimsby	Lancaster
101 Sqn	Ludford Magna	Lancaster
103 Sqn	Elsham Wolds	Lancaster
150 Sqn	Hemswell	Lancaster
153 Sqn	Scampton	Lancaster
166 Sqn	Kirmington	Lancaster
170 Sqn	Hemswell	Lancaster
300 (Polish) Sqn	Faldingworth	Lancaster
460 (RAAF) Sqn	Binbrook	Lancaster
550 Sqn	North Killingholme	Lancaster
576 Sqn	Fiskerton	Lancaster
625 Sqn	Kelstern	Lancaster
626 Sqn	Wickenby	Lancaster

5 *Group*

9 Sqn	Bardney	Lancaster
44 Sqn	Spilsby	Lancaster
49 Sqn	Fulbeck	Lancaster
50 Sqn	Skellingthorpe	Lancaster
57 Sqn	East Kirkby	Lancaster
61 Sqn	Skellingthorpe	Lancaster
83 Sqn	Coningsby	Lancaster
97 Sqn	Coningsby	Lancaster
106 Sqn	Metheringham	Lancaster
189 Sqn	Fulbeck	Lancaster
207 Sqn	Spilsby	Lancaster
463 (RAAF) Sqn	Waddington	Lancaster
467 (RAAF) Sqn	Waddington	Lancaster
617 Sqn	Woodhall Spa	Lancaster
619 Sqn	Strubby	Lancaster
627 Sqn	Woodhall Spa	Mosquito
630 Sqn	East Kirkby	Lancaster

Bibliography

Bennett, Air Vice-Marshal D C T, *Pathfinder* (Sphere Books Ltd, London, 1958).

Bishop, Patrick, *Bomber Boys: Fighting Back 1940–45* (Harper Press, London, 2007).

Blake, Ron, Hodgson, Mike and Taylor, Bill, *Airfields of Lincolnshire since 1912* (Midland Counties Publications, 1984).

Bowyer, Chaz, *For Valour: The Air V.C.s* (William Kimber & Co. Ltd, London, 1978).

Charlwood, Don, *No Moon Tonight* (first published by Angus & Robertson, Australia, 1956).

Currie, Jack DFC, *The Augsburg Raid* (Goodall Publications, London, 1984).

Delve, Ken, *The Military Airfields of Britain: East Midlands* (The Crowood Press Ltd, Marlborough, 2008).

—— *The Source Book of the RAF* (Airlife Publishing Ltd, Shrewsbury, 1994).

Delve, Ken and Jacobs, Peter, *The Six-Year Offensive* (Arms and Armour Press, London, 1992).

Falconer, Jonathan, *The Dam Busters: Breaking the Great Dams of Western Germany 16–17 May 1943* (Sutton Publishing Ltd, Stroud, 2003).

Finn, F, *Lincolnshire Air War 1939–1945 Book Two* (Control Column Publication, 1983).

Franks, Norman, *Claims to Fame: The Lancaster* (Arms and Armour Press, London, 1994).

Green, Peter, Hodgson, Mike and Taylor, Bill, *Wings over Lincolnshire* (Midland Publishing, Leicester, 1994).

Halfpenny, Bruce Barrymore, *Action Stations 2: Military Airfields of Lincolnshire and the East Midlands* (Patrick Stephens Ltd, Cambridge, 1981).

Halley, James J, *The Squadrons of the Royal Air Force and Commonwealth 1918–1988* (Air-Britain (Historians) Ltd, Tonbridge, 1988).

Hancock, T N, *Bomber County: A History of the Royal Air Force in Lincolnshire* (Lincolnshire County Council, 1978).

Ingham, Mike, *Air Force Memorials of Lincolnshire* (Midland Publishing Limited, Leicester, 1987).

Jacobs, Peter, *Bomb Aimer Over Berlin: The Wartime Memoires of Les Bartlett DFM* (Pen & Sword Books Ltd, Barnsley, 2007).

—— *The Lancaster Story* (Arms and Armour Press, London, 1996).

Middlebrook, Martin, *The Battle of Hamburg: The Firestorm Raid* (Cassell & Co, London, 1980).

—— *The Berlin Raids* (Viking, the Penguin Group, London, 1988).

Middlebrook, Martin, and Everitt, Chris, *The Bomber Command War Diaries: An Operational Reference Book 1939–1945* (Penguin Books, London, 1990).

Musgrove, Gordon, *Pathfinder Force: A History of 8 Group* (first published by Macdonald & Jane's, London, 1976).

Otter, Patrick, *Lincolnshire Airfields in the Second World War* (Countryside Books, Newbury, 1996).

—— *Maximum Effort: The Story of the North Lincolnshire Bombers* (Grimsby Evening Telegraph, 1990).

Rolfe, Mel, *Looking into Hell: Experiences of the Bomber Command War* (Arms and Armour Press, London, 1995).

Searby, John, *The Bomber Battle for Berlin* (Guild Publishing, London, 1991).

Sweetman, John, *Bomber Crew: Taking on the Reich* (Abacus, London, 2004).

—— *The Dambusters Raid* (Arms and Armour Press, London, 1990).